THE TRACTION LIBRARY™

GETTING EVERYONE IN YOUR COMPANY ON THE SAME PAGE

TRACTION: GET A GRIP ON YOUR BUSINESS
Strengthen the Six Key Components® of your business using simple yet powerful tools and disciplines.

FOR EVERYONE

GET STARTED:

ROCKET FUEL: THE ONE ESSENTIAL COMBINATION
Dive into how the Visionary and Integrator duo can take their company to new heights.

FOR VISIONARIES & INTEGRATORS

GET A GRIP: AN ENTREPRENEURIAL FABLE
Follow this fable's characters as they learn how to run on EOS® and address real-world business situations.

FOR THE LEADERSHIP TEAM

WHAT THE HECK IS EOS?
Create ownership and buy-in from every employee in your organization, inspiring them to take an active role in achieving your company's vision.

FOR ALL EMPLOYEES, MANAGERS & SUPERVISORS

HOW TO BE A GREAT BOSS!
Help bosses at all levels of your organization get the most from their people.

FOR LEADERS, MANAGERS & SUPERVISORS

THE EOS LIFE
Learn how to create your ideal life by doing what you love, with people you love, making a huge difference, being compensated appropriately, and with time for other passions.

FOR ENTREPRENEURS & LEADERSHIP TEAMS

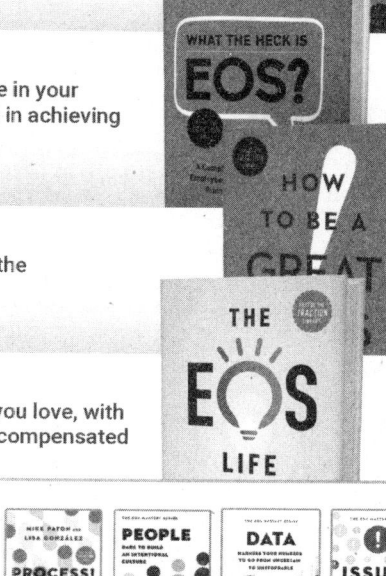

THE EOS MASTERY SERIES
Dive deeper into each of the Six Key Components for more masterful execution.

EOSWORLDWIDE.COM/TRACTION-LIBRARY

PRAISE FOR *ISSUES*

"*Issues* is built on a proven model with clarity around the next steps to grow your business. The approach drives improved communications, creates a transparent organization, and builds the foundation for the most important result: growth."

—Rhoda Olsen, vice chair of the board of directors for Great Clips, Inc.

"I've personally witnessed how Sue Hawkes's guidance through the EOS process is beneficial and impactful, and with coauthors Mark O'Donnell and Jill Young, she expands on this careful and strategically sound approach in *Issues*. One of the most organized and insightful people I've ever met, Sue's clear communication style makes learning this process even easier."

—Merrilee Kick, founder and former CEO of BuzzBallz/Southern Champion LLC

"Issues are the invisible friction that slows down greatness. In *Issues*, Hawkes, O'Donnell, and Young show you how to unleash the full potential in your team, making each day more effective and each quarter more profitable. Your human capital is your most valuable capital and Hawkes, O'Donnell, and Young's wise words help you tap its full potential."

—Lewis Schiff, chairman of the board of Birthing of Giants and author of *Business Brilliant*

"*Issues* resolution has always been THE ISSUE! This book is a wonderful set of principles that (applied diligently!) can move any business forward."

"Entrepreneurs don't lack ambition; they get stuck in messy issues. With decades of EOS wisdom, O'Donnell, Hawkes, and Young show you exactly how to work through them—quickly, decisively, and collaboratively—so your team grows stronger with every challenge. Consider this your guide to turning friction into fuel."

"*Issues* strips away the noise and shows what actually works. O'Donnell, Hawkes, and Young offer a grounded, real-world system for solving problems quickly and running a healthier, more aligned organization."

"I've seen firsthand how EOS helps leaders across the roofing industry tackle challenges head-on. *Issues* brings that same clarity and energy, offering practical tools that transform frustration into momentum and growth. This book reflects Hawkes, O'Donnell, and Young's commitment to building high-trust teams and solving problems fast—an invaluable resource for any organization striving for greatness!"

"There is a reason that the Issues List takes 60 minutes of the weekly L10. If a company can identify the key issues and quickly solve them, it is on the winning path. O'Donnell, Hawkes, and Young show you how to do that very thing. This book demystifies the EOS Issues List and turns it into your team's most powerful problem-solving weapon—clear, practical, and immediately usable. A must read for any leader who wants fewer distractions, better decisions, and a team that actually solves problems instead of just talking about them. Leaders who truly put their people first will find in these pages a practical way to face issues together and move everyone forward."

—David Mann, managing partner and cofounder of The Firefly Group

"I've seen over and over that you will never get the right people in the right seats if you don't first get great at solving issues. *Issues* gives leaders the missing muscle: the courage, tools, and discipline to surface the real people issues, cut through the "nice," and make clear, right-seat decisions for the greater good of the company. If you're serious about building a team of A-players in every seat—not just rearranging the accountability chart—this book will show you how to remove the friction that's holding your best people (and your business) back."

—Jonathan Reynolds, CEO and Visionary of Titus Talent Strategies

ISSUES

ISSUES

REMOVE FRICTION,
FAST TRACK YOUR GROWTH, AND
IGNITE YOUR GREATNESS

MARK O'DONNELL,
SUE HAWKES,
AND JILL YOUNG

WITH DAVID MOFFITT

BenBella Books, Inc.
Dallas, TX

BenBella Books, Inc.
8080 N. Central Expressway
Suite 1700
Dallas, TX 75206
benbellabooks.com
Send feedback to feedback@benbellabooks.com

BenBella is a federally registered trademark.

Printed in the United States of America
10 9 8 7 6 5 4 3 2 1

Library of Congress Control Number: 2025046892
ISBN 9781637748671 (hardcover)
ISBN 9781637748688 (electronic)

Copyediting by James Fraleigh
Proofreading by Ashley Casteel and Martha Gallant
Text design and composition by Aaron Edmison
Illustrations by Q Hawkes
Printed by Lake Book Manufacturing

Special discounts for bulk sales are available. Please contact bulkorders@benbellabooks.com.

To Rachel, Ava, Nora, and Quinn—my greatest teachers in life. Without your love and support, none of this would be possible. And to every entrepreneur who dares to solve their issues and make the world a better place.

—Mark O'Donnell

For my family, who remind me daily what truly matters— especially Kevin, my husband, partner, and the finest person I know—and for every leader courageous enough to face the real issues with heart and clarity, paving the path to freedom.

—Sue Hawkes

To all the leaders and coaches who obsess about solving issues. Thank you for adding ease to our world!

—Jill Young

CONTENTS

FOREWORD

I once wrote an article entitled, "My Greatest 'AHA' After 2,000 EOS Sessions." Its purpose was to get to the heart of what makes a business great. Not just okay. Not even merely good. Truly great.

Those 2,000 EOS sessions represented almost 14,000 hours in a session room with more than 135 teams. After all of that time, the answer was 100 percent clear to me (and still is). A great company is the by-product of a strong Leadership Team. Period. There isn't even a close second.

That naturally leads to a follow-up question. What do great Leadership Teams have in common? I defined seven characteristics that I had observed:

- They Have Rock Stars in Every Seat on the Leadership Team
- They Are 100% on the Same Page with the Vision and Plan
- They Speak One Language
- They Are Open and Honest
- They Are Fanatical About Resolution

- They Treat Each Other as Equals
- They Possess the Secret Sauce (they love each other)

Of those seven, this book goes to the absolute core of two of them. Here's how I described them in my article:

Great Leadership Teams Are Open and Honest: *The most successful companies have Leadership Teams that are comfortable with conflict. They don't hold back, they call out every issue, and they comfortably discuss them until they are resolved in one sitting.*

Great Leadership Teams Are Fanatical About Resolution: *A strong Leadership Team, after calling out all of the issues, is fanatical about resolving them. They typically solve 5 to 15 issues every week in their weekly meeting and 30 per quarter in their quarterly planning sessions, regardless of whether it's a people issue, a new idea, an opportunity, or a business problem. For strong Leadership Teams, issues never linger.*

The book you hold in your hands travels deeply down the path of exactly how the Leadership Team of a business can become the kind of team that never lets issues linger. As my friends and colleagues Mark O'Donnell, Sue Hawkes, and Jill Young say right from the start: The biggest epidemic that plagues businesses is a failure to solve issues fast and permanently.

That "fast and permanently" part matters. A big part of my passionate drive to understand and teach the world the art and science of running a truly great business meant creating powerful tools that leaders could apply efficiently under daily pressure. Tools that would drive true, lasting change.

Too many businesses settle for the flavor-of-the-month "solution," only to see it fall flat when they grasp for the next thing the following month. Out of my drive to give business owners something that would actually work came EOS (the Entrepreneurial Operating System). Through *a lot* of trial and error, I discovered the Six Key Components that every great business needs to strengthen to be great. Today, EOS has a global following that includes more than 850 EOS Implementers and an organization helping hundreds of thousands of companies around the world run on EOS.

The Issues Component was born in part from my observation that leaders were exhausting and demoralizing themselves and their entire organizations by letting the same problems hang around. Doing so kills the spirit, kills profits, and sometimes even kills the company.

I created the Issues Solving Track a year and a half into working with clients. After 18 months of watching multiple teams discuss the heck out of everything but rarely identify the root issue or solve it, the solution hit me like a flash of light. In a fit of rage, as I lovingly like to describe it because it was frustrating to watch. I urged the team to take a few steps back and follow the Identify-Discuss-Solve (IDS) process for solving their issues, and it worked. Over and over again. Every time. This book is that process, and I'm grateful to Mark, Sue, and Jill for bringing it to life. It was a true joy to be the book's first reader. They nailed it!

Mark, Sue, and Jill rightly encourage you to not just think about the Issues Component tools, not just to implement them half-heartedly, but to completely obsess over them.

This returns to my earlier description: The best Leadership Teams are fanatical about resolution, meaning that they obsess about resolving issues fast and permanently. And the simple but powerful tools outlined in the following seven chapters are your shortest distance to growing your own fanatical team of resolution experts. Spend time with this book and deeply absorb its lessons, then obsess about making it happen in your own company.

The payoff will be enormous. Great Leadership Teams live a life of freedom. This freedom isn't only financial; it's that wonderful feeling of freedom that happens when you choose to truly be in charge of your business.

The only other choice is to allow problems, outside forces, and the whims of luck to be in control. That choice will exhaust you and your business. Ironically, when you take full responsibility for your issues, you'll find your luck increases too.

That's really what it comes down to: Choose freedom through the discipline of issue solving, or choose the oppression and anxiety of chronically unresolved issues.

The authors have masterfully laid out every practical tool and mindset you need to make the leap to greatness. The only thing none of us can do is make the choice for you.

Gino Wickman
Author of *Traction* and *Shine*
Creator of EOS®

CHAPTER 1

· · · · · · · · · · · · ·

THE SECRET GREAT
TEAMS KNOW

This book has the cure for the biggest epidemic that wears down businesses: **a failure to solve issues *fast* and *permanently*.**

This epidemic is serious enough that some businesses die from it—unfortunately, we've witnessed it. For other businesses, it may not be quite fatal, but it destroys growth and momentum. By failing to confront issues productively, these organizations just muddle along, never reaching their potential, stuck hitting the same ceiling over and over.

Not solving issues does obvious harm to profits. As bad as that is, this epidemic spreads beyond your bottom line. It also can create a demoralized culture of dissatisfaction and misery within your team.

WHAT DO WE MEAN BY "ISSUES"?

Right from the start, it is crucial to define clearly what we mean by the word "issues." Is it just another word for problems?

Problems are part of it, but it's much more than those. **Issues are problems, challenges, obstacles, and *also* opportunities and new ideas that are worth your attention.**

Think of issues as any kind of friction or trapped energy that, if solved, would unleash more growth and make your team and your business demonstrably better, either immediately or over time. One good way to find your most significant issues is to consider what (or who) is consistently ticking you off. But issues aren't just about what is frustrating you. Issues also refer to ideas and opportunities that you see and capitalize on.

It's also important that you adopt a particular mindset when you hear the word "issue." It should inspire a detached approach, so that you come at an issue with more objectivity and less emotion. Obstacles, problems, and opportunities aren't reasons for getting upset. Rather, say, "It's just an issue," and solve it.

The book *Traction* nails it: "It's normal to have issues. The sooner that you can admit that you have them and not view that as negative thinking or some kind of weakness, the faster you will move forward."

For your people, leaving issues unsolved can feel like being stuck in an echo chamber. The same meetings that solve nothing. The same individuals bouncing off each other repeatedly, without anything ever changing. In these conditions, is it any wonder many businesses struggle with a lack of enthusiasm or proactive energy?

Forget innovation—people are just trying to survive another boring meeting or weather another customer crisis. New challenges are hard to tackle when you can't even solve the old ones.

If that all sounds kind of dark, it can be. Businesses can crash and burn over one big issue they refused to face and solve. Failing to conquer issues permanently can start to feel like the famous definition of insanity: *"doing the same thing over and over again and expecting different results."* This can make day-to-day experiences within a business miserable.

Here's the thing, though. This situation is far from hopeless. There are teams who have learned the tools that solve issues fast and permanently. And if that's true—and it certainly is—then that means any team can learn to do it too. It just takes the right methods and the courage to implement them.

It also means that the teams that *do* solve issues fast and permanently are absolutely crushing it compared to those who are caught up in the epidemic. In fact, businesses that master the method and practice of solving issues are downright recession proof, bulletproof, and any other proof you can dream up. Every leader should be hungry and passionate to discover the mindsets, tools, and methods that give them this game-changing edge.

STOP HIDING

At the heart of the failure to solve issues fast and permanently is an all-too-common behavior that can be summed up as various kinds of hiding.

- **Hiding from the truth** about what is at the root of an issue.
- People **hiding from accountability** or the risk of new ideas.
- Leaders **hiding from clarity** behind indecisiveness and disorganized messages.
- **Hiding from what you really want** and being afraid to say it out loud.

At the most basic level, this epidemic begins with individuals hiding, then grows into a whole team that has evolved into a habit of hiding from the hard stuff. Obstacles get ignored or covered up.

Teams shy away from new ideas or listening to the thoughts of others. New opportunities for growth remain hidden because no one wants to stick their neck out and be wrong.

Many business cultures teach their people to *not* reveal issues: Don't let anyone know you screwed up. Fix it before people find out. And never say bad things about other teams or areas of the business that you don't oversee. This is particularly common in corporate environments, but the truth is, this is common across all types of organizations.

Butt-covering is a learned behavior, and unless a Leadership Team specifically and intentionally creates an issues-solving culture that's open, honest, and transparent, most companies will drift in the direction of avoidance. Even the best people in your organization will not risk being blamed for exposing challenges or proposing new ideas if the culture is discouraging. The meaning of the word "dis-courage" is to *move away* from courage. When your company culture isn't open, honest, and transparent, you're literally pushing your people away from courageously confronting challenges.

Some individuals will use every opportunity to keep deflecting and ducking no matter the culture. If your culture is stuck in hiding mode, you're extending an invitation for these people to stay under the radar forever, undermining the entire organization. But once you know how to transform your company into an *issues-solving machine*, there is no longer anywhere to hide.

Would you say your business is filled with people who cooperatively and obsessively drill down to the root of the issue, always with the Greater Good of the company as the first priority?

Or does it often seem like motives are a lot more mixed, with too much butt-covering and complaining eating up time and motivation?

One great way to diagnose your company is to examine the state of your meetings.

ANOTHER MEETING . . . UGH

Ask most people about the quality of their meetings and you'll get an earful, and it won't be positive. Do the following descriptions sound familiar?

- Your meetings seem more about endlessly describing problems, challenges, and opportunities, but not solving them. Meetings become a rehashing of stories or an exercise in excuses and justifications that keep us stuck.
- There are a lot of "if only this" or "if it weren't for that"–type statements. The bulk of your discussion focuses on the surface-level symptoms. Rarely are the meeting participants in danger of coming close to directly confronting the root of the issue.
- The person who should be leading the discussion, the one most responsible for the issue under scrutiny, hangs back and never seems to contribute anything meaningful toward a real solution.

- Meeting participants rush right to throwing out guesses and seeking consensus instead of starting by searching for the root of the issue at hand.

Eventually one of three things happens to put a meeting out of its misery:

- The leader of the meeting gets frustrated with the lack of progress toward a solution, and announces a snap decision on the spot. You can be sure a "solution" like this will not be permanent. *Or . . .*
- The discussion loses steam and everyone agrees on a vague idea about what might make the issues better, or maybe just agrees that more information is needed. Nothing is settled and there are no clear, concrete next steps. *Or . . .*
- The meeting ends because it runs out of time, but then there is a "meeting after the meeting" where a smaller number of like-minded people gather to complain about other attendees and talk about the real issue in a more honest way.

MEETING MISERY

Here are some sure signs that your business isn't using meetings to solve issues fast and permanently:

- People often sit there thinking, "This meeting is a waste of time."
- A typical thought is, "We could have handled this with a quick email exchange."

- Pre-meetings happen frequently, where the real decisions are made, and the actual meeting turns into a box-checking exercise.
- There are too many people in meetings because leaders aren't taking control of who should really be in the room.
- The real issues are being discussed quietly by smaller groups after the meeting.
- Your meetings have a town hall atmosphere. Everybody feels like they need to stand up and spout, even if they have nothing much to say.
- You often get to the end of what feels like a productive, lively meeting but then realize no decision has been made and no specific action will result.
- Your meetings are low-energy affairs: dull, stale, and *boring*. (Hint: This is because no one is actually bringing forward or confronting issues.)
- One or two people tend to dominate the conversation, often repeating themselves and bickering unproductively.
- Most of all, many meetings make everyone think, "I've gone to this same meeting over and over and over again!"

If any of this sounds familiar, your business is likely caught up in the epidemic: You aren't confronting and solving issues.

How much human energy is being wasted because your meetings aren't efficient? Are monotonous meetings crushing your team's passion, innovation, and hunger for growth? How many team members are losing confidence because their ideas and input never seem to change anything?

In the coming chapters, we will show you *exactly* how to change this forever, but first let's take a step back and get the 10,000-foot view.

EOS AND THE ISSUES COMPONENT

The concepts and tools you will learn in this book about solving issues fast and permanently are proven and tested. This isn't theory; what we teach is part of the Entrepreneurial Operating System® (EOS®) that has been used by tens of thousands of businesses.

Created by founder Gino Wickman, EOS teaches businesses how to improve the "Six Key Components®" of an organization: Vision, People, Data, Issues, Process, and Traction. This book is all about strengthening your Issues Component®.

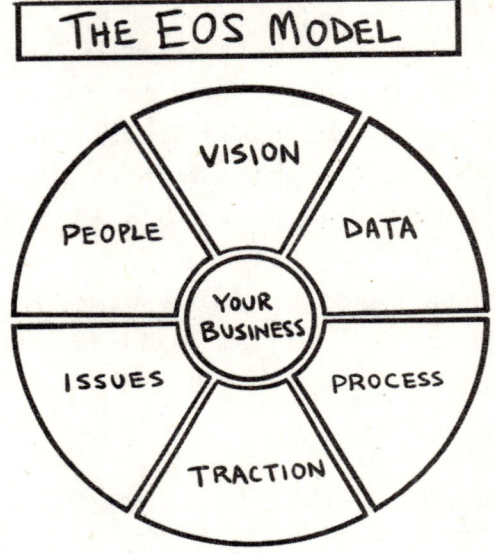

AN EOS OVERVIEW

EOS is a simple way of operating a business. It's a complete system, full of timeless concepts and simple, practical tools that help owners and leaders get what they want from their businesses. Through painstaking study and years of trial and error, Gino Wickman discovered how to help Leadership Teams resolve the hundreds of common issues facing an entrepreneurial company.

What Gino found was that each and every common issue was caused by weakness in Vision, People, Data, Issues, Process, and Traction—what we call the Six Key Components of any business—as illustrated in the EOS Model.

Whether implementing the EOS Tools and concepts on their own or with the aid of an EOS Implementer®, Leadership Teams follow a Proven Process to strengthen each of these Six Key Components.

A strong **Vision Component®** means everyone in the organization is 100 percent on the same page with where the company is going and exactly how it plans to get there. A strong **People Component®** means you've clearly defined what a "great person" means in your unique business and you're great at attracting and retaining them. A strong **Data Component®** means you're running your business on a handful of numbers that give you an absolute pulse on your business, predict future results, and help you make better, faster decisions.

A company with a strong **Issues Component®** (our topic in this book) can solve issues as they arise and make them go away forever—rather than letting them linger for weeks, months, and sometimes even years. A strong **Process Component®** is about getting the most important things in your business done the right and best way every time. And finally, a strong **Traction Component®** is about instilling discipline and accountability at all levels of the organization so that, everywhere you look, everyone is executing on the vision day in and day out.

The journey to implement EOS is a journey to strengthen *all* Six Key Components. Many leaders mistakenly believe that they can solve all the issues in their business just by working on one or two of the components, but we know from experience that becoming 80 percent strong or better in each of the Six Key Components will help you run a truly great business. To get a clear picture of your organizational strength in each of the Six Key Components, visit organizationalcheckup.com.

You can also learn more about EOS by reading *Traction: Get a Grip on Your Business* by Gino Wickman.

There's no need to be an EOS expert to gain value from this book, but those who'd like to learn more can visit www.eosworldwide.com. To be sure, even if you're unfamiliar with EOS, the fact that you've been interested enough to read this far is a sign that you will certainly understand and benefit from the concepts and tools in the pages that follow.

THE HEART OF THE ISSUES COMPONENT

At the most fundamental level, the Issues Component is about creating a discipline for meeting your impurities, challenges, ideas, and opportunities head-on and solving them so they go away forever.

How do you create that discipline? The entire book will explain the "how" in full, but in this chapter we will lay the foundation for getting to the core of issue solving. Here's the good news: The discipline of solving issues fast and permanently requires you to master only two tools.

Any team committed to doing this *can* do it, and it will be transformative. Understanding the process is relatively simple, and then it just takes consistent application of what you have learned. The harder part is finding the courage to keep applying it, especially when squarely facing the "tough stuff."

THE TWO TOOLS

The Issues List—This is a shared document where the team can list the business's problems, challenges, obstacles, opportunities, and new ideas so they can then be addressed efficiently and productively. Using actual lists is crucial. You absolutely can't keep your issues in your head and expect it to work! We cover this topic in depth in chapter 3. For now, just know that you will be amazed at the relief and clarity an Issues List will bring to you and your organization. The relentless worries and vague ideas that keep waking you up at 2 AM will finally stop.

The Issues Solving Track—This powerful tool consists of three steps: Identify-Discuss-Solve (IDS). Once you get your entire organization to put on their IDS "glasses," you will ignite greatness—everyone will begin to see things differently. Teams who execute the steps well, and in the right order, win over and over again. First they prioritize the most important issues to handle first. Then they make sure they spend enough time on the Identify step. Too many teams discuss and discuss and discuss endlessly before they have even identified the root of the issue. Chapters 4, 5, and 6 explain this in detail.

While the tools themselves aren't hard to understand, it can be easy to get off track because it's human nature to avoid what we perceive as negative. A vital guide to keep you on track is the 10 Commandments of Solving Issues.

THE 10 COMMANDMENTS OF SOLVING ISSUES

From *Decide! The One Common Denominator of All Great Leaders* by Gino Wickman

1. THOU SHALT NOT RULE BY CONSENSUS

On a healthy team, where the vision is clear and everyone is on the same page, eight out of ten times, everyone will agree with the solution to a problem. However, sometimes they won't, and someone needs to make the final decision. That someone is the leader. Consensus management doesn't work, period. Eventually, group-consensus decisions will put you out of business. When the leader makes the final decision in these situations, not everyone will be pleased, but as long as their voices have been heard and if the team is healthy, they can usually live with it. From there, you must always present a united front moving forward.

One of the worst cases of consensus management that I've experienced was a company being run by its next generation of family members. The company's growth was stagnant, and some tough decisions needed to be made to restore profitability. In our first few sessions, every time a hard decision needed to be made, either the team would retreat out of fear of hurting someone's feelings or some-one would say, "Let's vote." This waffling had been going on for years. They were some of the nicest people you could ever meet. Yet they would come to the next session complaining about all of the same issues and how nothing was working. After a year of forcing more openness and a few very uncomfortable sessions for some people, one of the owners finally stepped up as the company Integrator and started to make the tough decisions. Finally, the ship started to turn around for them.

In countless cases I've observed when the team was divided, if the leader had gone along with the majority, it would have been the wrong decision. In a *Fortune* maga-zine issue on decision-making, Jim Collins, the author of *Good to Great*, is quoted as saying that in his years and years of research, "No major decision we've studied was ever taken at a point of unanimous agreement."

2. THOU SHALT NOT BE A WEENIE

The solution is often simple. It's just not always easy. You must have a strong will, firm resolve, and the willingness to make the tough decision.

3. THOU SHALT BE DECISIVE

In the classic book *Think and Grow Rich*, Napoleon Hill cited a study that analyzed 25,000 people who had expe-rienced failure. Lack of decision, or procrastination, was one of the major causes. In contrast, analysis of several hundred millionaires revealed that every one of them had the habit of reaching decisions promptly and changing them slowly. It's less important what you decide than it is that you decide ... so, decide!

4. THOU SHALT NOT RELY ON SECONDHAND INFORMATION

You cannot solve an issue involving multiple people without all the parties present. If the issue at hand involves more than the people in the room, schedule a time when everyone can attend. One client calls these "pow-wows." When someone brings him an issue involving others or secondhand information, he says, "Time for a pow-wow," and pulls everyone involved together and solves it.

5. THOU SHALT FIGHT FOR THE GREATER GOOD

Put your egos, titles, emotions, and past beliefs aside. Focus on the vision for your organization. You will cut through the candy-coating, personalities, and politics. If you stay focused on the Greater Good, it will lead you to better and faster decisions.

For instance, the Integrator of a $7 million international distribution company explains, "The toughest decision I ever made was to present an aggressive budget that would impact the partners' compensation considerably over the next one to two years. I worked on the budget the entire fourth quarter and went back and forth many times before finally deciding to go for it the night before the meeting. At our annual meeting in January, I presented it. It was a tough sell, but I knew it was the right thing to do for the Greater Good of the company. It was a tough meeting and took a few hours, but they agreed. Since I received the partners' buy-in, we went from having our worst year to having our best year, and next year looks like more of the same. I plan on having generous partner distributions by the end of this year and moving forward."

6. THOU SHALT NOT TRY TO SOLVE THEM ALL

Take issues one at a time, in order of priority. What counts is not quantity but quality. You're never going to solve them all. The faster you understand that, the better your odds are of staying sane. Solve the most important one first, and then move on to the next.

You'll also find that when you do this, some of the other issues on the list will drop off because they were symptoms of the real issue that you solved.

7. THOU SHALT LIVE WITH IT, END IT, OR CHANGE IT

This is a great lesson from my dad, who is a very successful entrepreneur and one of my greatest mentors. In solving an issue, he teaches that you have three options: You can live with it, end it, or change it. There are no other choices. With this understanding, you must decide which of the three it's going to be. If you can no longer live with the issue, you have two options: change it or end it. If you don't have the wherewithal to do those, then agree to live with it and stop complaining. Living with it should, however, be the last resort.

8. THOU SHALT CHOOSE SHORT-TERM PAIN AND SUFFERING

Both long-term and short-term pain involve suffering. You have a choice with all of the issues you face. A great rule of thumb that makes this point is called "36 hours of pain."

If you're wrestling with a tough decision, whether it involves strategy, customers, or people, and you're procrastinating because of the prospect of it being painful, hopefully this will give you some motivation. During the growth of Niche Retail, Tyler Smith kept someone around for a year too long because he was having a really hard time making the decision to let him go. What made the problem really tough was that this person had been with them through the early years. The company had outgrown him, though. He was aware of this, and, over time, his attitude had soured. The Leadership Team finally realized that there was simply no other option. The person was no longer right for the organization. As a result, after much anguish and soul-searching, Tyler finally made the tough decision to let him go. A couple of days later, Tyler called me and shared this term that's now a staple in my work with clients: 36 hours of pain.

The months, weeks, days, and hours leading up to the termination were painful, but after that, he realized it was one of the best decisions he had made for the Greater Good of the company. He couldn't understand why he hadn't done it sooner. The work environment was so much better and less tense for everyone. Other employees thanked him for making the tough decision. He experienced all that pain for a year, when in hindsight he could have experienced only 36 hours of pain, probably for both parties. Incidentally, the terminated gentleman is now doing well and pursuing his passion. The decision was best for all.

Solve your problem now rather than later. The fear of doing it is worse than actually doing it. Choose short-term suffering.

9. THOU SHALT ENTER THE DANGER

The issue that you fear the most is the one you most need to discuss and resolve.

In tough times, people tend to freeze. When you're afraid, your brain actually works against you. Research now shows us that when we are fearful, we use the back part of our brain, the amygdala.

That's our primal brain, developed thousands of years ago to protect us from predators. It's responsible for our fight-or-flight response, which doesn't serve us well when solving business problems.

You must shift to the prefrontal part of the brain, the rational and critical thinking part. That will serve you well in decision-making situations. The way to do this is to simply list all of the things that are worrying you: all of the problems, concerns, and fears. You can do this as an individual during your Clarity Break [which those running on EOS will recognize] or as leadership in one of your meetings. Being open and honest will enable you to confront and solve your critical issues and get moving forward again.

10. THOU SHALT TAKE A SHOT

Taking a shot means that you should propose a solution. Don't wait around for someone else to solve it. If you're wrong, your team will let you know. Sometimes the discussion can drag on because everyone is afraid to voice a solution even though someone may have it right on the tip of his or her tongue. Often, a team will discuss an issue for far too long. They'll be stuck and no one will be offering solutions, when suddenly the quietest person in the room might speak up and suggest something. There might be a silence, then someone says, "That's a good idea" and everyone agrees. Don't be afraid to take a shot. Yours might be the good idea.

Note to the reader: We will be sharing these commandments individually throughout the book where it connects with the topic at hand to reinforce their importance.

HOW THE ISSUES COMPONENT ALIGNS WITH THE OTHER KEY COMPONENTS

As just described prior to the 10 Commandments of Solving Issues, EOS is a complete system of Six Key Components. But do any of the six stand out above the rest in importance?

The short answer is no. To elevate one component unnaturally above the others would give the wrong impression. That would imply that you could or should sacrifice working on one component to get better at another.

All six components work together to get a business humming at maximum growth and breaking through ceiling after ceiling. They are complementary components, not competing ones.

Think of the six components as something like an orchestra. An orchestra will break down into chaotic sound unless every section plays its proper part. The EOS components work together as a system with none elevated above the other, just like a perfectly aligned orchestra. This is similar to your Core Values (which we'll cover more in chapters 5 and 7), where none are more important than another.

While acknowledging this truth, we also say this: The Issues Component has a special relationship to all the other components, as well as to your business's growth and long-term success.

A few examples demonstrating what we mean:

The **Data Component** serves as an early warning system in your business, alerting you to challenges, problems, and opportunities. But all by itself, it only points to issues; it doesn't solve them.

Repeated missed deadlines and unmet expectations indicate weaknesses in your **Process Component**. But no process has ever been known to fix itself. It takes a business that is great at confronting issues to go to the root of why a process is breaking down and then solve it permanently.

If you're unclear on your target market, where you're going or how you'll get there, you have an impurity within your **Vision Component**. That lack of clarity needs to be worked through using the Issues Solving Track.

What if the key tasks your people are accountable for (we call these to-dos and Rocks) are not getting you any closer to your goals? This is something inside your **Traction Component** that you can Identify-Discuss-Solve.

Sometimes a repeated problem keeps pointing to an issue with one or more people in your organization. Before you can take action that *truly* solves a **People Component** issue, you have to correctly identify what is going on at the root. Is it a person in the Wrong Seat? Is it someone who doesn't align with your Core Values and doesn't belong in your organization at all? You need to be great at solving issues, with the courage to drill down and find the right answer.

The crucial point is this: If your team doesn't get good at solving issues, you won't make progress in the other components. Your team's time, energy, and enthusiasm will be wasted discussing symptoms. You will never get to the heart of issues, and that will make lasting progress in the other components impossible.

IMPORTANT ISSUES INSIGHT Based on our experience working with tens of thousands of businesses, 80 percent of your issues have to do with your People or Process Components. Teams struggle the most with solving issues for the long-term Greater Good in these two areas.

Addressing People Issues can be especially tough because we often allow a lot of emotion to cloud our thinking in this area. Some refer to this as the "heart trap"—the tendency to let emotional discomfort prevent tough but necessary decisions. It will undermine accountability with your teams.

Process can be challenging because it takes a bulldog commitment to dig into the details to figure out where it's breaking down. The teams who solve People and Process Issues are rewarded with remarkable results.

NO ISSUES? THEN YOU *REALLY* HAVE ISSUES.

If you have read to this point, and you think you don't have any significant issues in your business, then we know you have at least one issue: denial!

When a team claims to have few or no issues, they might as well be under a huge, flashing sign screaming, "WE DEFINITELY HAVE ISSUES!"

A business with no issues . . . are you kidding?! Without issues, your business is dying from a lack of ambition and a lack of care. If you don't have problems, challenges, ideas, and opportunities, then a reasonable deduction is  that you also have no goals. Because if you have goals you haven't reached, there must be a gap. There is *always* friction between where you are and where you want to go.

If the gap between where you are and where you want to be isn't pushing your team to work through ideas and problems, the only explanation is that you're fooling yourself with fake goals that aren't challenging your organization. In chapter 3, we'll help you discover ways to uncover issues and get them on a list.

HOW TO FAST-TRACK GROWTH

The Road to Massive Breakthrough Success Is Paved with Solved Issues.

The subtitle of this book (*Remove Friction, Fast-Track Your Growth, and Ignite Your Greatness*) sums it up. The key to fast-tracking growth is to remove friction. Once you and  your organization build this muscle, it flips a switch and ignites something special for your team and your future. The ability to solve issues will make your team and your business truly great.

And all you have to do to spark this revolution is become obsessed with your Issues List and the Issues Solving Track.

GO AHEAD, GET COMPLETELY OBSESSED

There are a few simple skills, tools, and methods that must come together if a company is to become exceptionally proficient in solving issues fast and permanently. But if we were to choose one word to summarize and describe what separates the mediocre from the great, it would be this: OBSESSED.

Obsessing is usually considered a bad thing, and often for good reasons. There are certain areas in life and business where obsessions are destructive. Going down rabbit holes or focusing on the wrong things is the bad side of obsession.

But there are exceptions, and issues are absolutely an exception.

In fact, consider this book permission to become completely obsessed with creating a team that is world class at solving issues fast, and in a way that those concerns never return. Obsession, in this context, is not a flaw but a critical virtue, and it can ignite a total transformation. Obsession implies total focus and commitment, and when you have that, momentum naturally follows.

Massive growth is one of the greatest rewards for this kind of obsession. But it will not be the only one. As the team "gets it," you will see your people grow tremendously right along with your organization. The right people—the ones you want on your  team—will be energized and passionate about working toward the Greater Good of the company. New leaders will emerge as the company becomes more open, more honest, and more transparent. You will see people step up and truly solve issues that push the business forward by leaps and bounds.

This doesn't mean a conflict-free journey filled with roses and colorful balloons. Solving issues at their core often involves uncomfortable conversations with people and changing outdated processes, but this discomfort is a necessary part of growth. It still requires conflict, but now instead of battling each other, your team is fighting together for the Greater Good.

The top companies in the world have masterful teams obsessed about solving issues. And when they get complacent and stop solving issues fast and permanently, they set themselves up for a coming crash. The most legendary business leaders are certainly not afraid of being obsessed with solving issues.

The best part about this kind of relentless focus? You don't need to learn 100 tools or methods. You don't need to go earn an advanced business degree or learn complicated formulas.

You have two tools to master, and they are both simple to understand. Of course, as you know, simple is not the same as easy. But if you truly commit to using Issues Lists, and you obsess about using the Issues Solving Track, and you apply the 10 Commandments of Solving Issues, you will make game-changing progress in your business in a relatively short amount of time.

All you have to do is get completely obsessed about it.

ISSUES ARE A GIFT

Many of us learned at a young age to avoid problems and failures at all costs. Or if you couldn't avoid them, at least don't draw attention to them or yourself. In short, we learn to hide. Recall from the beginning of this chapter that this hiding often becomes a habit, and it prevents us from solving issues. You have zero chance of truly solving challenges if you can't even look at them honestly.

BUT WHAT IF . . .

. . . you trained your organization to be *grateful* for issues? That when obstacles, challenges, ideas, and opportunities arise, you and your team would see them as the path to continuous growth. **Issues are the raw material for growth.** Issues will always be a catalyst—a negative catalyst if you hide from them until they blow up in your face, or a positive catalyst if you put them on an Issues List and then successfully IDS them.

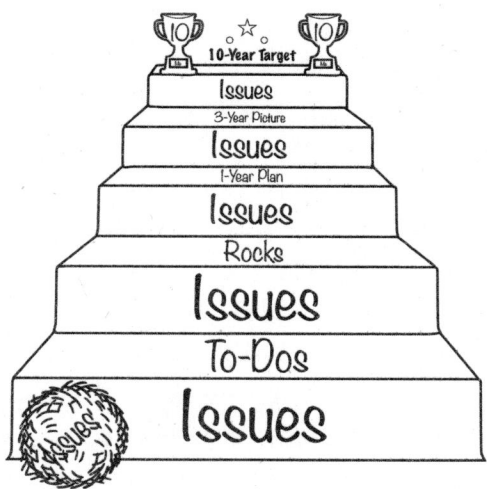

The best leaders know that issues are a gift to be grateful for, because they can be transformed into fuel for growth. Every obstacle, barrier, impurity, opportunity, and idea should challenge and excite entrepreneurial teams, not make them shrink back in fear!

AND WHAT IF . . .

. . . you and your team simply acknowledge that issues will always be part of growth? In other words, you all understand that issues are in some sense *always the work*. Daily, you will face multiple challenges, and they don't stop the next day. Instead of treating issues as something to tolerate, why not just get remarkably good at solving them? Problems and challenges are going to happen either way, so why not roll up your sleeves instead of saying "woe is us"?

AND, FINALLY, WHAT IF . . .

. . . your company became so mature at solving issues that it kept growing, and your issues only grew too? That means it's time to celebrate that you're playing on a bigger field, with higher-level challenges and massive opportunities. Why did you become an entrepreneurial leader if not to keep knocking down barriers, staring down the next challenge, and imagining all that could be?

When you can fully embrace the mindset of "I'm excited we have issues, because it means we're growing!" then you will ignite greatness. You'll be growing externally with more profits, and growing internally because your team will become razor sharp from the discipline of attacking issues at the root.

Great teams realize issues catalyze growth. They learn to resolve everything that stands between them and their vision of the future. When you and your team become energized by and grateful for having issues to solve, you will have truly unlocked the secret fuel that powers all great teams.

THE CULTURE YOU MUST BUILD
IF YOU WANT THIS TO WORK

Before we dive into the nitty gritty of the tools themselves, it's important to understand that the commitment to the tools isn't enough. The tools only work when they are used in a company that promotes a sincerely open and honest culture.

If your people don't feel secure enough to address things openly, the impact of the tools will be greatly lessened. If you have a repressive, fear-based culture, these tools will be useless until you switch to an intentional culture rooted in abundance and openness.

How to encourage that kind of honesty is the subject of our next chapter.

* * * * * * * * * * * * * * * * *

Solving Issues in Real Life

Mower: "We Did What Would've Taken Us 10 Years to Do Without EOS"

Mower is an award-winning, full-service marketing, advertising, and public relations company.

In August 2022, Mower went through a huge transition. Up until that point, Eric Mower was the owner of the company, one he had originally joined in 1968.

After 57 years, Eric decided it was time to transition Mower to become 100 percent employee owned through an ESOP (Employee Stock Ownership Program). Then a few months later, he became executive chairman of Mower and Stephanie Crockett became the CEO.

"We had a transition going on with the ESOP," Stephanie said. "Plus, the agency was weathering the storms of a very volatile advertising industry that tends to swing with ups and downs in the economy. We weren't in crisis, but it made sense to bring in EOS as we faced all this change."

As they began working with EOS Implementer Sue Hawkes, one of the things that became clear was that Mower had people who were not in the right place within the organization. "We had a lot of people that were awesome humans but that weren't in the right role. But up to then, nobody was really doing anything about it."

It was in dealing with these people issues that Identify-Discuss-Solve was particularly useful.

"I think IDS has been especially beneficial for people issues. We have always been a very kind organization," Stephanie said. "We're very polite, and honestly had sometimes kept situations going out of kindness and love, but that's not necessarily dealing with the tough challenges when performance is not where it needs to be, or there is not a fit."

The structure of IDS and the culture of openness and honesty it inspires helped address these difficult issues without the company losing its heart.

"Using IDS and the structure has enabled us to be kind, loving humans, but also have the space to say what needs to be said and really address challenges," she said. "Always with heart of course, but actually dealing with them and not just brushing them under the rug."

Stephanie continued: "We can be clear with each other that this people issue is something we need to fix. It's either someone in a Wrong Seat, or they are the wrong person and need to find the way to the right organization for them."

IDS has also given them the means to capitalize faster on potential opportunities and ways to serve their clients better. "We sometimes have to deal with current events that impact a broad range of our clients, and we need to be proactive in figuring out how to help them. In the past when that would come up, an email would have gone out to the team asking who wants to tackle this. It would have been kind of ad hoc and maybe taken weeks."

Now the group deals with these kinds of issues in the weekly meeting and comes out with clear to-dos and actionable items, and everyone knows who is responsible for what. Instead of taking weeks to react to an opportunity that requires fast action, the plan is rolling when the weekly meeting is done.

Stephanie has also noticed that the team is now willing to be more direct in dealing with issues.

"There is definitely more of a comfort level in having fierce conversations and calling something out when it's not right," she said. "We move faster, fix things quicker, and move on opportunities we want to act on." She added that the whole team can see this. "This has permeated through the organization. I can see more urgency and focus throughout the company."

Stephanie said that staying focused during IDS is something they still work on, but they are committed to it. They post the IDS framework right at the top of the Issues List so they are constantly reminded to stay on one issue at a time and remain on topic.

"We sometimes have the process begin with story after story, and either myself or our Integrator has to say, 'Hey, wait a second, let's remember what we are trying to identify. What are we solving? Who is this for?' We are using the IDS framework to make our meetings as efficient and valuable as possible."

One thing that has been satisfying for Stephanie and the team at Mower has been to look back on all that has been accomplished.

"As we were in the middle of all the change, you are just using the tools and structure and getting it done," Stephanie said. "Looking back, we've improved so many things. We created and implemented processes, fixed problems with people, and got through all of it."

She added: "We did all that through the EOS structure in a way that would've taken us another 10 years to do without it."

CHAPTER 2

· · · · · · · · · · · · ·

OPEN AND HONEST

Is your business "a NICE place to work?"

We hope not.

At least not if you define "niceness" as an absence of healthy conflict. We define nice as "**N**othing **I**n me **C**ares **E**nough to tell you the truth." For a business that wants to be truly alive, growing, and thriving, nice should never be the goal.

So don't ask yourself if you have created a NICE place to work. Ask: Is your business a place where the team trusts each other enough to tell the truth, the whole truth, and nothing but the truth? The goal should be honesty even when it's uncomfortable. *Especially* when it's uncomfortable.

The reason you need honesty is because **all progress starts with telling the truth**. Reality has a way of eventually crashing in if you ignore it. To solve issues permanently, you have to be in touch with the reality of what is actually going on.

At EOS, open and honest is a baseline requirement. This is an expectation we explicitly communicate to every client at the start of every session we run. Open and honest is at the very root of how we make a difference inside organizations.

Most people nod along with the idea of being open and honest *in theory*. But implementing those behaviors in real time and in the real world is harder than just agreeing with the idea.

We should also add: When we say stop worrying about being "nice," we of course don't mean you should be cruel or act like a bully. The best advice is simply this: Be kind and be clear. More on this as we progress through the chapter.

A visual might help in getting a deeper understanding of this. Take a look at the following page.

Let's begin with the idea of trust.

Most businesses will have small pockets of trust within their organization. Maybe John trusts Sofia, Sanjay, and Amara. But he does not trust Dylan, Kai, or Megan.

These little alliances don't add up to trust. They are just factions. Chances are good that John, Sofia, Sanjay, and Amara are "nice" to the others in a meeting, but then get together later at the water cooler to say what they truly think. That's not solving issues with trust. It's gossip.

Trust is *everyone* in the business working together toward the Greater Good. This doesn't mean that everybody has to be best friends or that people won't naturally "like" some people more than others.

THE CULTURE ALIGNMENT MATRIX[IP]

	Low (HEALTHY) CONFLICT High

TRUST (High → Low)

High Trust, Low Conflict

Elephant in the Room

- Polite avoidance
- Empathetic erosion
- Afraid to tackle the issues
- False security
- Living in the illusion
- Comfort trap
- Losing so slowly it feels like winning or incremental growth
- NICE—Nothing In me Cares Enough (to tell you the truth)—not kind
- Peace at any price
- Gossip
- End runs

High Trust, High Conflict

Fearless Accountability

- Spicy growth
- Constructive tension
- Dynamic debate
- Disagree and commit
- Assume positive intent
- Right Person, Right Seat (RPRS)
- Healthy conflict
- Challenge-driven growth
- Invested for the Greater Good
- See feedback/healthy conflict as energy
- Comfortable being uncomfortable

Low Trust, Low Conflict

Silent Sabotage

- Pretentious peace
- False harmony
- Toxic passivity
- PC pretentiousness
- Going through the motions
- Quiet quitting
- Calm before the storm
- Ignore and do the minimum
- Unmotivated
- Victimized
- Blaming
- End runs

Low Trust, High Conflict

Dog Eat Dog

- Toxic work environment
- Us vs. them
- Backstabbing
- House of cards
- Walking on eggshells
- Everyone for themselves
- Burning bridges
- Turf wars
- Chaos
- Overwhelming emotions
- Fractured culture
- Doomloops

Low ← **(HEALTHY) CONFLICT** → High

It does mean there is a genuine care and concern for the worth and value of each individual and their right to be heard.

If you don't have that, you can't claim to be high on the trust continuum.

GREATER GOOD?

You may have noticed that whenever we refer to the Greater Good, we capitalize it. That's because when we say Greater Good at EOS Worldwide, we're not talking about some loose concept that sounds vaguely pleasant. We mean something precise. Here is an excerpt from *People: Dare to Build an Intentional Culture* that explains it:

DEFINING THE GREATER GOOD

At EOS Worldwide, our yardstick for how we serve others well is always pursuing the Greater Good of the organization. Here's the simple formula:

GREATER GOOD = EVERY WORD OF THE V/TO

X

GENUINE CARE AND CONCERN

The V/TO (Vision/Traction Organizer) is a way to boil down your vision into a two-page document that gets your vision out of your head and down on paper. Besides bringing clarity for the Leadership Team, it will also allow everyone else in your organization to see where you want to go . . .

> *The second part of the formula is Genuine Care and Concern, a multiplier to Greater Good being achieved. It means exactly what it says: that in all your actions, behaviors, and words, you have Genuine Care and Concern for every team member.*
>
> For more on this topic, see the *People* book, especially chapter 2, "What's Love Got to Do with It?"

What does a low-trust atmosphere look like in practice?

Living in the Dog Eat Dog quadrant is probably the most miserable place you can work. Here all dysfunction has broken out into frequent open hostility. Rivalries and backstabbing at the leadership level create a toxic house of cards that will eventually land the business in crisis mode. Before that happens, though, a lot of turnover will happen. The best people that care the most will flee the fastest.

What makes the difference between this ugly situation and Fearless Accountability (the quadrant where you want to be)? In the low-trust version, everyone's in it for themselves. In the high-trust version, everyone is in it for the Greater Good of all.

If your business is trending toward or living in the Dog Eat Dog quadrant, consider that an emergency. It will only continue to spiral downward without a firm commitment from the Leadership Team to change it. Everyone in a leadership position needs to take responsibility for shifting the unhealthy dynamics. Someone needs to go first and show the courage and vulnerability to be open and honest.

In some cases, the damage of a Dog Eat Dog culture has reached the point where no one is willing to take the first step or can't even see a way that it could be done. In situations like this, strongly consider getting some outside help to facilitate immediate and drastic change.

If Low Trust/High Conflict is the most miserable, the Silent Sabotage quadrant is the most lifeless. Here there are fewer fireworks; people get worn out more slowly. It is a tense game of maintaining a false face and keeping a superficial peace.

Everyone is still out for themselves, but instead of open warfare, it is "quiet quitting" while doing the bare minimum. You may even fool yourself about this reality because you're losing so slowly it feels like you're winning.

Leaders with this kind of team need to ask themselves how to inject passion back into the business and get people to care again. Accountability needs to be restored, and anyone who can't get on board needs to go.

Let's shift to the conflict continuum. You might be tempted to think that the best quadrant is Elephant in the Room. In this environment, people seem to genuinely like each other, and there is little fierce debate. Recalling the beginning of this chapter, you could say "it looks like a nice place to work."

The problem is that a low-conflict organization is rotting from the inside out from a lack of honesty. By the time you realize where you are, your business might be in a world of trouble.

Companies need a reality-based search for the truth of what is happening internally in the business and externally in its industry. That requires high energy and passion, which inevitably stirs the pot of conflict. The absence of strong, healthy debate is a red flag that things are just way too nice and crucial issues aren't being confronted.

HIGH-TRUST/HIGH-CONFLICT QUADRANT: THE PLACE TO BE

At first, hearing that you want a high-conflict workplace might sound counterintuitive. Don't you want a peaceful, harmonious workplace with everyone working together in seamless collaboration? Part of the issue comes from the word "conflict" itself. People assign different undertones to it.

Some people hear "conflict" and they immediately think of a person who loves fighting for the sake of fighting. Or they associate it with unproductive interpersonal antagonisms that devolve into things like screaming matches. That's unhealthy conflict, and we of course aren't encouraging that.

However, a lot of people shy away from productive conflict because they are afraid to risk not being liked, or because finally confronting issues will often expose conflicts surrounding a key person on the team that have festered beneath the surface, sometimes for years. Better to just label conflict "always bad" than to deal with the truth.

COMMANDMENT #5 FOR SOLVING ISSUES: THOU SHALT FIGHT FOR THE GREATER GOOD

Put your egos, titles, emotions, and past beliefs aside. Focus on the vision for your organization. You will cut through the candy coating, personalities, and politics. If you stay focused on the Greater Good, it will lead you to better and faster decisions.

LESS CONFLICT = MORE FRICTION

By avoiding conflict between people and ideas, you're leaving in place choke points that are killing opportunities for growth. Those choke points are the friction that you need to eliminate so you can fast-track progress and profits.

Conflict is the full airing of that friction, exposing it to the light of day for healthy discussion and debate, and producing aligned solutions. It may sound a little strange to say less conflict = more friction, but it's true: The more you avoid passionate discussion and debate, the more bottlenecks you build.

The key point is your business will never be what it could be without the dynamic debate and constructive tension of a healthy-conflict culture. Imagine the growth possible if everyone was intense enough to bring their best selves and work it out together, knowing that at heart, everyone sincerely wants what is best for the Greater Good.

However, without the glue of high trust, your business will not survive high conflict. That's the crux of the dilemma.

GET SPICY

If you're really struggling to get past negative connotations around the word "conflict," try shifting your thinking to "spicy" instead.

Adding spice to food makes it tastier and better, but it also creates some edginess in the dish. Spicy makes for a better meal while introducing an element of surprise and risk.

Ask yourself: Do your meetings typically include some spicy debate? Does your approach to solving issues include the spice of transparent truth telling?

If you choke on the word "conflict," then try getting spicy.

BUILDING TRUST

You might be thinking, "I get it, but how do you create trust?" It's not like you can go in one day and suddenly announce to the team, "I hereby declare that from now on, we're going to trust each other!" and everyone magically begins to do it.

It's true that you can't wave a trust wand, but you can make a conscious effort to implement ideas and concepts that build trust. It can happen faster than you think, especially if leaders walk the walk. Author Simon Sinek popularized the concept that leaders should "eat last" but lead from the front on difficult missions. Being first to take on challenges but last to take credit is a clear message for your team, one they will pick up on and emulate. The rest of this chapter is dedicated to ways you can develop a high-trust environment (or, if you have one already, to make it even better).

ASSUME POSITIVE INTENT

One particularly helpful concept is "assuming positive intent."

Almost all of us have had past experiences of getting burned, betrayed, or bullied. It can naturally lead us to adopt a "prove I can trust you" attitude toward people and situations.

This is especially true if someone suggests an idea different from our own or proposes something that potentially threatens our perceived turf. The natural instinct is to get defensive and assume the worst.

Instead, try intentionally assuming positive intent and watch how situations transform into something better.

For example, say a new sales manager observes early in her tenure that leads are leaking from the sales funnel due to a lack of follow-up. She had a terrific experience with a particular CRM system at a previous company that solved this exact problem. She puts forward the idea of subscribing to this same CRM.

One of the top veteran performers on the sales team is immediately opposed. He does just fine using his own tracking method, thank you very much. He thinks there's nothing that needs fixing other than his fellow sales colleagues becoming more accountable.

This is a situation ripe for conflict; the only question is whether it will be healthy or counterproductive. In a low-trust culture, this will become a turf battle, with each "side" trying to recruit their own faction. Whether the CRM is actually what is best for the Greater Good is at best a secondary concern.

In a high-trust environment, positive intent is assumed. In this scenario, the sales manager doesn't assume that the veteran sales-person is opposing change to sabotage her. She listens carefully to what he has to say, and it spurs her to reflect on whether the CRM is a good solution for her current team. She either comes up with reality-based facts to bolster her case or she drops the idea.

If the salesperson is assuming positive intent, he will carefully listen to the sales manager as she describes her experiences with the CRM. If he has concerns about the accountability of fellow team members, assuming positive intent might make him consider that one of the reasons the sales manager wants the new CRM is to increase accountability.

None of this is to say that everyone's intent is always 100 percent pure. However, starting with assuming the best allows you to listen better while finding collaborative solutions that serve the Greater Good.

If you want to build trust, it is crucial that the owner (or CEO or Visionary), president (or COO or Integrator), and the entire Leadership Team model this behavior. It creates a positive feedback loop where assuming positive intent becomes the habit.

Making it standard will also reveal anyone on the team who can't live out this principle. When most of the organization becomes high trust, those who remain crouched in a "protect myself first" posture are exposed.

GET INTENTIONAL ABOUT LISTENING

In the CRM example, you might have recognized that the word "listen" came up a lot. That's not an accident. If you're struggling with trust and solving issues, start modeling active listening from the leadership level.

We are all partners in helping each other get what is inside our heads out and into the world where it could make an impact. The better a listener someone is, the more they can help draw out what the other person has to say. Poor listening means we're not fully absorbed in what another is saying, but instead are inside our own head working out our own take. It happens all the time.

Practice silencing the chatter inside your own skull as others share their ideas and issues. Make it a habit to take a beat and let what they say permeate your thoughts. Lead others with this example and they will benefit and take action.

SHOW YOU ARE LISTENING

"Active Listening: show genuine interest in your direct report by giving them your full attention, maintaining eye contact, nodding when appropriate, and paraphrasing or summarizing their points to demonstrate you understand."
– From *People: Dare to Build an Intentional Culture*

STRONG BELIEFS, LOOSELY HELD

What if you believe you *are* actively listening, but yet never seem to change your mind? Chances are high that you aren't actually absorbing any new data or challenging your own ideas.

Leaders need to walk a fine line here, and it is perhaps best expressed with the phrase "strong beliefs, loosely held" (sometimes attributed to Amazon founder Jeff Bezos).

The idea behind this expression is that as a leader, you cannot be a reed swaying back and forth every time the wind changes direction. You need firmness of purpose and thought-out beliefs.

But the opposite danger is getting so caught up in your strong beliefs that you can become blind to that data and to reasons that don't support your own ideas. Your bias for your own beliefs can become almost invincible. This is where the "loosely held" mindset can help you be open to changing your mind.

"Loosely held" can also mean accepting that you got something wrong and admitting when the data confirms it. As a leader, you are willing to put your neck out there and make a tough call. As part of the deal, you accept that you won't always be right, and that when you're wrong it isn't about you personally.

Demonstrating your commitment to aligned solutions other than your own will help your team trust your leadership even more and give your entire culture a growth mindset.

TAMING DRAGONS

If the thought of conflict still sounds to you like unproductive fighting, here is another image that may reveal its true nature: You're **not** battling each other, you're taming dragons together.

At EOS Worldwide, we have been sharpening an open, honest, and vulnerable culture for a long time. If you observe our meetings

when we are hashing some-
thing out fully, you might be
taken aback by the directness
we have with each other. An
outsider might say, "That looks
absolutely brutal."

From the inside, it feels
different. It might look like
combatants on opposite sides of the table, but because we focus on
the Greater Good, from our perspective we are fighting the dragon
standing in the way of us and our future.

That dragon is whatever issue we are addressing that is causing
friction and holding us back from getting what we want as a team.
The healthy debate of conflict and no-holds-barred truth telling is
the fastest and most effective way to get to the root of an issue. We're
going to be obsessive and aggressive because it's that important. Our
collective future is on the line.

Healthy conflict means pursuing the root of an issue without
fear holding you back from saying what you want to say. Think of
it as a "no stone unturned" commitment where all perspectives are
necessary. The result is a richer, more diverse conversation that leads
to the truth or the best possible answer.

Author Patrick Lencioni likes to call out pursuing "Truth
with a capital T" as a cornerstone of effective teamwork and
decision-making. It means seeking objective reality or the best possible decision for the team or organization, rather than prioritizing
individual preferences, egos, or political agendas. Unfiltered debate
uncovers truth. This is what we mean by fighting together to tame
dragons.

BOOK RECOMMENDATION: *THE FIVE DYSFUNCTIONS OF A TEAM*

One of the best resources for creating a team rooted in trust is Patrick Lencioni's classic work, *The Five Dysfunctions of a Team*. The five dysfunctions are absence of trust, fear of conflict, lack of commitment, avoidance of accountability, and inattention to results. Through the story of a fictional CEO, Lencioni demonstrates how these issues manifest and derail teamwork.

The dysfunctions build on one another, starting with a lack of trust, where team members avoid vulnerability, preventing open dialogue. This leads to fear of conflict, which stifles healthy debate and results in lack of commitment and unclear decisions.

This is a great book for a deep dive into how the lack of trust creates a dysfunctional team afraid of conflict, commitment, and accountability. It all adds up to disappointing results.

DIAGNOSING WHO IS STRUGGLING WITH OPENNESS AND HONESTY

As you start shifting to more open, honest, and transparent communication, some people won't want to make that leap, often (but not always) because the issues being exposed center around that person. Or because they are afraid to risk building the trust necessary to work through the tough stuff.

We recommend observing the behavior of people in the room when tough things are being discussed.

Example: The Leadership Team is working hard in a meeting to improve operational issues. The person in the Operations leadership seat is the one contributing the least. Sometimes you can actually see them physically shrink back. This is a red flag that the person is struggling with honesty and accountability.

Pay close attention to body language and behaviors. If someone's posture becomes closed during a conversation, gently inquire about their internal dialogue; for instance, "What conversation are you having in your head right now?" This approach can unlock hidden emotions, allowing the team to address underlying issues directly.

Sometimes you will be able to coach someone into more trust and honesty. Tell them your only expectation is that they lower their guard, open their mind, and let whatever is running through their head fly out of their mouth.

Some people still will not be able to get on board with this approach, and it will become clear that the person isn't the right fit for your company. In this case, be courageous enough to help them leave the organization and free them to find a place where they will thrive.

Seeking openness and honesty has to be a priority for your culture. If a person can't be open and honest, they are holding the whole team back, and perhaps the entire company.

PSYCHOLOGICAL SAFETY

Another way to think of trust is as psychological safety. Accountability is crucial, but not when used as an excuse for bullying tactics, blaming, or shaming. That behavior shuts people down because they will avoid drawing any attention to themselves. They'll do just enough to stay off your radar.

We recommend making a conscious effort to foster trust by allowing team members to voice their opinions without fear in the spirit of contributing to a shared outcome. Be sure to include key elements of psychological safety, such as the following:

- **Acknowledging Contributions:** Celebrate input and bravery, even when the final decision doesn't align with someone's suggestion.
- **Constructive Conflict:** Use conflict as an opportunity to strengthen your team. It may cause a few emotional bruises along the way, but remember that "scar tissue" is stronger than original tissue.
- **Addressing Disruptive Behaviors:** Call out gossip and passive aggression directly to maintain a healthy team culture.

POSITIVITY ISN'T ALWAYS POSITIVE

Many voices in the business world advocate for the creation of a "company culture of positivity."

Some define this as a culture with an abundance mindset, rooted in an overall belief that any obstacles can and will be conquered, and that living your best life is completely possible. If that's how positivity is being used, sign us up, because that matches the EOS Life perfectly! (The EOS Life is doing what you love, with people you love, making a huge difference, being compensated appropriately, and with time for other passions.)

However, we have witnessed many teams who say they have a culture of positivity, yet what they mean is that anything with a whiff of negativity should be suppressed. From their perspective, conflict equals negativity, and negativity is the opposite of positivity, and therefore no conflict is allowed.

This is just another way we delude ourselves into not tackling tough concerns, dealing with thorny people issues, and facing reality.

Foster a genuinely positive sense of abundance? Definitely. Hide behind a fake idea of positivity? Count us out.

TRUST REQUIRES TRUST

Everything mentioned up to this point will help sow the seeds of a team who trusts one another. Assuming positive intent, taming dragons, psychological safety, and all the rest can transform a culture if practiced with consistency. But there is also a "chicken or the egg" quality to trust.

Does trust come first, or do you have to risk first in order to be able to trust? As Ernest Hemingway said, "The best way to find out if you can trust somebody is to trust them." Having trust allows you to take risks with other people, and taking risks with other people builds trust.

The *American Heritage Dictionary* defines trust as "firm belief in the integrity, ability, or character of a person or thing; confidence or reliance." Notice that the key word in the definition is "belief." Trust is not trust without the willingness to take on a certain amount of risk and to just go ahead and believe.

A team that trusts each other has many benefits, and one of the biggest is that it allows you to risk making many more mistakes but with a lot less fear. When everyone believes you're acting for the Greater Good, no one will use slip-ups as an excuse to attack.

COMMANDMENT #9 FOR SOLVING ISSUES: THOU SHALT ENTER THE DANGER

The issue that you fear the most is the one you most need to discuss and resolve.

Being open and honest will enable you to confront and solve your critical issues and get moving forward again.

The groundwork has been laid. It's time to dive into the tools. Used correctly, the tools provide a way to mute the kind of conflict that is unhealthy while sharpening the kind of healthy conflict that is productive and necessary.

Solving Issues in Real Life

Latitude and Aroris Health: The Power of Open and Honest

Latitude is a strategic creative agency that helps build and activate brands in the marketplace, providing branding and marketing services for retail and other industries.

Aroris Health increases revenue for private healthcare practices across the United States through payer negotiations and strategic implementation.

When COVID-19 hit, Krista and Jeremy Carroll's agency, Latitude, faced an existential threat. After laying off 75 percent of their staff, Jeremy was ready to shut it down. "I asked Krista to shut it down, and she said we weren't going to do that."

At that point they made a crucial decision: either go all in on EOS with a professional Implementer or close their doors for good.

"If it doesn't work, we're probably going to have to shut down our business," Jeremy told Troy Schuette, their EOS Implementer, during their first meeting.

Founded in 2009, Latitude had grown into a strategic creative agency that helped build and activate brands in the marketplace. While much of their work focused on retail, they also provided branding and marketing services across various industries. By 2013, they had discovered EOS and opted to self-implement with modifications.

The business continued to grow, but then the pandemic

struck. It exposed weaknesses that had been developing beneath the surface of their apparent success.

"Self-implementation didn't work for us," Jeremy said. "The business did continue to grow, but we did not have a framework for running it and scaling it. When we hit different crises, we didn't really know how to manage them effectively."

Krista notes that it wasn't until after they went all in on EOS implementation that they truly understood one of the big challenges at the center of the business.

"It was powerful to understand the Integrator and Visionary roles from reading *Traction*," she said. "Jeremy is a very pioneering-type Visionary, and I was playing the role of Integrator. But Troy helped me see that I was a Visionary too."

She continued: "Essentially we were struggling with two Visionaries with pretty distinct visions of the company. That was creating a lot of tension."

As this picture became clearer through working the tools and implementing EOS fully, a big change was made.

"We got to a point where I asked Krista if I could step away from the business," Jeremy said. "She had the tools, the team, and the confidence to let me step away. She has been running it ever since with her Leadership Team."

This freed up Jeremy to launch Aroris Health, a business he decided also would run on EOS.

Other positive changes happened when Latitude went all in on EOS, especially the empowerment of the team that came from using the Issues Component tools.

"We had to start to build a culture where putting issues on the Issues List isn't tattling or being negative or throwing people under the bus. It's doing your best due diligence for the organization and it's really helping each other," Krista said. "Exposing issues is going to let everybody thrive. But it can be the hardest thing, especially in Minnesota where there can be this kind of 'nice passive-aggressive' sort of thing going."

Krista decided to model an open and honest approach for her team. "I intentionally put issues on the list where I was the bottleneck," she said. "I admitted I wasn't able to respond timely enough for everyone to get what they needed from me."

But this vulnerability opened a productive conversation about processes and delegation that ultimately empowered the entire agency.

Jeremy echoes how empowering it is for the entire team to learn the value of openness and honesty when addressing issues.

"In other organizations, accountability tends to come from the top down, and in a lot of them, everything is under the owner's thumb," he said. "But if you do EOS right, everyone knows their role and they're accountable to themselves and their teammates."

He added, "It's really a culture of empowerment that EOS promotes. It's a constant reminder and encouragement that every team member is part of the solution, and that we need them to make us grow. Their voice is valued at the table."

Both businesses have found strength and growth as they committed fully to this path. It also had another huge benefit for the Carrolls.

"As husband-and-wife leaders running a business during a really tragic time in the world, EOS helped us make sense of our business and it kept us from putting too much on our marriage," Jeremy said. "It's scary to look back and think of what it could have done without EOS."

Krista agreed, and then Jeremy continued: "I know there's a lot of husband-and-wife leaders out there, and I'd like this to be an encouragement to them. Learning these tools elevated us during a dark time in our business that could have spilled over into too much pressure on our marriage. This is the place to start to make better sense of your business, which helps you have a better marriage too."

CHAPTER 3

· · · · · · · · · · · · · · ·

THE ISSUES LIST

The first Issues Component tool might sound almost too simple—it's a list?

Yes, it's simple. But it's a game-changing step. It takes impurities, challenges, and opportunities that are vague and free floating and converts them into something you *have to deal with*. It is the crucial transition that takes obstacles and ideas trapped inside your head and gets them objectively down on paper. **It is the first step in a disciplined process** where you will work through challenges and ideas using the Issues Solving Track.

It's also more than a list. If you do it right, it's also an aid to analysis, prioritization, and preparation.

We'll dive deeper into that, but first some practical definitions: **An Issues List is a shared document for a team to surface challenges, friction points, obstacles, opportunities, ideas,**

impurities—anything that is unresolved. Most organizations have it as an online document accessible by all relevant team members.

We often refer to the Issues List in the singular, but the reality is there are two types of list, one long term, one short term. Here are the key differences between them:

Long-Term List
- If an issue can't be solved immediately (or within the next 90 days), it belongs on the long-term list. Think of it as the "parking lot."
- For businesses running on EOS, this is the Issues List you will find on your Vision/Traction Organizer (V/TO). It's a dedicated space within the V/TO for long-term company challenges that are not immediate priorities but need to be addressed in the future. Examples include new product ideas, technology needs, office relocation, or capital requirements.
- This list is for items you are shelving to ensure focus on the most pressing priorities for the current 90-day period.

Short-Term List
- If an issue covers a high-level, strategic item that needs to be resolved within the week or this 90-day period, it belongs on the Issues List you use during your Leadership Team's weekly meeting (for those running on EOS, this is your Level 10 [L10] Meeting).
- Issues that belong on this list include things like off-track company Rocks, off-target Scorecard numbers, important client worries, key employee concerns, or process and system challenges impeding your business right now.

- Leadership meetings should address these issues while pushing department-level concerns to their respective teams, ensuring the focus remains on what matters most at the organizational level.

Please also note that you should have department-level Issues Lists too. Each clearly defined team within the company should have their own Issues List to maintain their focus. Basically, if it's a team that holds its own meetings regularly, then it should have its own Issues List.

HOW TO GENERATE ISSUES FOR THE LIST

If you're already familiar with EOS, the tools from the other five components (Vision, People, Process, Data, and Traction) are the best place to begin. The tools will inevitably surface issues when used well.

For example . . .

Data—Scorecard: This is the tool for consistently measuring the metrics that matter. Some businesses create an excellent Scorecard, but then fail to react when it reveals challenges. If the Scorecard is off track for two weeks or more, get it on the Issues List.

Vision—V/TO: The first tool in EOS is the Vision/Traction Organizer. It gets your vision out of your head and onto paper and becomes *the* guiding North Star for the company while giving definition to the Greater Good. What issues are keeping

you from realizing the vision and plans in your V/TO? Get
them on the list.

People—Accountability Chart: The Accountability Chart is
a supercharged map of roles and responsibilities. It lists out the
"seats" in your business and clarifies five major roles for each
seat. A crucial question to ask when someone is in a seat: Do
they GWC (**G**et it, **W**ant it, and have the **C**apacity to do it) the
roles required? If the answer is no, that's an issue for the list.

Clarity Breaks and **Quarterly Conversations:** These are two
tools in the EOS Toolbox that create space and time and often
reveal ideas, opportunities, and challenges. Be on the lookout
for things that surface during these times.

Always remember that the Issues List is a living document.
Each of the six EOS components has several tools to improve some
aspect of your business. The system is an issue-generating machine,
and those issues are the raw material you use to grow. If you're doing
EOS well, you will have no shortage of fuel to power your business.

To come up with issues, it can also be helpful to think of the
ways you measure the success of your business, and how you deter-
mine if your progress is aligned with your vision. This will help you
surface challenges that belong on your list.

It's also important to remember not to overcomplicate this
process:

- You have goals, and then you have a gap between where
  you are and those goals. What's in the way of closing those
  gaps? Get it on the list.

- Your team is made up of people, which creates the need for training, or coaching, or separations. Get these on the list.
- Your business relies on finite resources of time, energy, and money. That must involve making decisions about trade-offs. Get them on the list.

In other words, how could you *not* have issues for the list?

If you catch anyone on your team claiming no issues, put this list of questions to them:

- What causes friction?
- What or who ticks you off?
- What could we do more effectively?
- What are we avoiding?
- What would act as a game changer for our team/business?
- How could we improve our processes?
- What could we do if we had unlimited resources (time, energy, people, money)?
- Where could I (our team/department/company) improve most?
- What skills/competencies do we lack?
- Who should we work with that we don't currently work with?
- What needs are underserved in our market?
- Where are we underutilized?
- Where are we at capacity?
- What needs to change to exceed our goals?
- Is there anything taking us off our Core Focus?
- What professional development do I/we need to grow into our future?

BRING TWO ISSUES

From the book *Traction*, here is another idea if the team isn't generating issues for the list:

A client shared a great idea that he used when he was having a hard time getting the people in his department to be open and honest in the identification and resolution of issues. For his next meeting, he made it mandatory that everyone bring two issues. If someone did not have two, he or she could not attend the meeting. He said it was the best meeting his team ever had. With the floodgates open, they are healthier than ever.

Note: As a general rule, you want 50 percent or more of your meeting to be used for IDSing a list, not for creating a list. But this idea can be helpful if your team is struggling early on with adding issues to the list.

WHEN IN DOUBT, GET IT OUT

When deciding what goes on an Issues List, beginners should start with this guideline: When in doubt, get it out of your head and on paper (the Issues List).

As you and your team get more comfortable and skilled at managing the list, you'll get a better feel for what belongs on there and what doesn't. But for now, there are good reasons to err on the side of capturing everything and then refining the list as you go.

A PSYCHOLOGICAL TRAP AND A PSYCHOLOGICAL BENEFIT

One common psychological hurdle to overcome is being afraid to add something to the list because you think you need to have a solution (or at least a hint of one) first. It makes many of us anxious to propose an issue for which we don't have an immediate answer. There is no control in that; it makes us feel vulnerable.

Of course, this is the entire point of adding something to the Issues List! It's for anything unresolved. If you knew what the cause and solution were, you would have solved it already. An Issues List is about what you're observing, what you're seeing on the surface. It doesn't mean you have a ready-made solution. Get vulnerable by putting it on the list.

Once that psychological trap is overcome, many people discover a psychological benefit.

All those hazy fears, ticking bombs, and potential opportunities are suddenly out of your head and on paper. You see the path leading away from the chaos of firefighting and moving toward the calm of prioritizing. For many leaders, the relief is almost immediate.

Of course, the follow-through has to happen for this to last. But once you take the first step of creating an Issues List and begin using it, you see a light at the end of the tunnel. This is the way to take the emotion and fear out of solving challenges. The whole team can shift focus from brush fires to tackling meaningful, high-impact issues systematically.

HOW MANY ISSUES ARE TOO MANY?

There is no one-size-fits-all ideal range for the number of issues you should have on your list at any one time. A few general rules of thumb could help, though:

- Too few issues is a much bigger red flag than too many. If you have hardly any issues, either you aren't using the list or you aren't pushing your business hard enough.
- As you get more adept at using the Issues List and the Issues Solving Track, your list will probably shrink. You'll get a better feel for what goes on the list and remove what is better addressed in another way or can be safely ignored.
- The list will also shrink as you get better at immediately seeing which issues all point to the same thing and can be merged into one challenge.
- At other times, the list will tend to grow. As teams prepare for quarterly meetings and annual planning, it's common for the list to expand.

ELIMINATING THE MISUSE OF AN "OPEN-DOOR" POLICY

We understand the intended benefits of an open-door policy. This is the management approach where leaders encourage peers and direct reports to bring their ideas, concerns, or feedback directly to them at almost any time. Transparency, trust, and a collaborative work environment are the aims, and those are all good things. As we made clear in chapter 2, openness and honesty are bedrock principles of a healthy culture.

In practice, however, an "open-door" policy can be misused. Its biggest problem is how much time it can cost with interruptions followed by unfocused conversations. "Do you have a minute?" quickly becomes 30 minutes or more. Those 30 minutes can also become a temptation to gossip. When the conversation finally ends, chances are you're no closer to a permanent solution, and now you have to spend energy refocusing on whatever you were doing before the interruption.

Another concern is that team members come in looking for solutions without first making an effort on their own. The leader is then pressured to come up with the solution for the team member. All of this adds up to an invitation for dysfunction.

The discipline of an Issues List can transform this situation. It makes little sense to have two people discuss an issue that should be approached with input by the entire team. Get it on the list.

Once the issue is on the list, it can be tackled in the weekly Leadership Team meeting. That will open up the debate to multiple perspectives and stop the gossip that can accompany smaller discussions.

Using an Issues List instead of the constant interruptions of "Got a minute?" is all about having the discipline to handle issues in the most effective way, with efficiency and structure. You can free up serious time and eliminate distractions. Do it and reap the rewards.

THE ALL-HANDS-ON-DECK EMERGENCY MEETING

Another common time waster is the meeting called suddenly because an urgent issue has surfaced. There may be *exceptionally rare* circumstances where this kind of meeting is justified and productive, but typically it reveals something else: that the company has failed to prepare and prioritize with an Issues List. This kind of "hot take" meeting often does more harm than good because people feel panicked and unprepared, and it can turn into a blame-game session.

There is nothing wrong with accountability, but these "Everyone in my conference room now" meetings lack the discipline and structure of an Issues List.

Tip: For more on how to make "offline" or quickly scheduled meetings more productive, see the "Offline Meeting Track" section in chapter 8.

MORE BENEFITS

CONFIDENCE TO SPEAK UP

Without an Issues List, many friction points may go unspoken, particularly on the front lines of your business. Not all team members are confident enough to bring up issues unless encouraged to do so.

Once a list is in place, the team has a structure for speaking up and pointing out challenges and new ideas, even if they can only see part of the issue. Friction that otherwise stays invisible too long gets surfaced because the Issues List is empowering your team.

SAFETY TO SHARE CONCERNS

For some, revealing issues can feel like "telling on" someone, being negative, or exposing yourself to retaliation. If someone is hesitant to bring up an issue, they need to remember the Greater Good. Sharing concerns isn't about attacking a person; it's about solving something that makes the organization stronger.

The Issues List makes it safer and simpler to share concerns. It is an objective, unemotional repository for concerns needing to be addressed.

NAMING AND TAMING THE DRAGONS

A good way to encourage more participation in calling out issues is to share with your team our earlier concept of fighting those dragons. Issues = dragons. And everyone works together to name and tame those dragons.

If you encourage this mindset, people can see the value of being willing to call out those dragons so they can be fought and tamed. It enhances team bonding by fostering an "us against the problem" mindset rather than gossip or blame-shifting.

OKAY, YOU HAVE AN ISSUES LIST . . . NOW WHAT?

Before you begin to IDS the issues on your list, we recommend each person on the team spend some time with it in preparation for the meeting. Strong teams take time to think about the issues before attending a meeting where they will IDS those issues. If you jump right to IDSing with a long list without some pre-thought, you're more likely to get frustrated.

In chapter 4, we will talk more about prioritizing and compartmentalizing the Issues List. For now, we want to give you some tips that can pay big dividends. These aren't required, but leaders and team members who take some extra pre-meeting time to prepare for IDS will be ahead of the game.

TWO QUIET MINUTES

At a minimum, consider taking two quiet minutes before (or at the beginning of) the meeting to review the list. What issues immediately stand out in terms of importance? Which ones have been frustrating you again and again? Which scare you? Which has the greatest impact for the organization? Which are time sensitive or mission critical?

Encourage your team to take this quiet time too. Even a small pause for reflection before attacking your Issues List will be helpful. The more you practice this, the better you will get at spotting patterns. Speaking of which . . .

MATCH GAME

As you read through the list, one of the things you might try is playing a version of the match game.

Let's say you have a list with 34 things on it. Look closer at it. Is it really 34 issues? Or is it 34 symptoms of what are actually 6 issues?

Sometimes it will be fairly obvious where symptoms are overlapping and pointing at the same cause. That *exact* cause will probably not be clear until you IDS it, but it will allow you to condense the list significantly.

If a bunch of issues are posing challenges or obstacles, you might begin to see a common thread among them. Think of it like this: Sometimes we have a bunch of fruit flies buzzing around, and we are trying to get rid of them one by one. Of course, the solution is staring us  in the face: Get rid of the rotten fruit! This is how it can be with an

Issues List. We are staring at a long list of individual fruit flies that are all pointing at the same root: the rotten fruit.

Another simple question to ask when consolidating an Issues List is, "How many issues on the list are essentially the same thing worded differently?" Because multiple people will be adding issues, chances are high that the list will have the exact same things called out from different perspectives. When you take the time to review a long list with a wide-angle lens, it would not be unusual for, say, a 60-issue list to drop by a third or half.

The other thing you may notice as you go through the IDS process is that when you solve one issue, several others may disappear along with it. This is a sure sign that your "issues" were in fact symp-

toms of the same issue, often pointing to one person or process. The more you practice IDS, the better you get at spotting these connections.

There may be some orphans on the list, too, things you can't quite link with anything else. Ask these two questions about such isolated issues:

- Is this even an issue? If so, what outcome is it keeping us from achieving? The answer may be either it isn't an issue, or it's not meaty enough to justify IDSing it. Strike it from the list.
- Does this appear to be a one-off issue, but it's really the tip of some dangerous iceberg? This question could open up something hidden that needs more attention.

PREPARATION

One last point before we dive into the nuts and bolts of the Identify step.

The Issues List is an extremely concise and productive way to prepare for a meeting. If you have been reviewing the list, of course you have already been preparing.

Take it a step further. Of the issues you have identified as the most important impact points, what thoughts do you have to share with the team that will be IDSing it with you?

What questions will you ask to get to the root?

Have you started to form "strong beliefs, loosely held" that you will test with the group?

What data is needed to properly Identify the root of the issue? How will you access that information so it's available prior to the meeting?

You will likely be able to come up with many more questions to help you prepare. Investing some time with your Issues List before the meeting will pay dividends as you move to the core of the IDS methodology: getting to the root of the issue.

Keep in mind that this "pre-work" is a suggestion, to be used especially if you're feeling overwhelmed by your Issues List. If it is helpful, use it, but never let it keep you from the main event: IDSing.

. . . .

Solving Issues in Real Life

Catco: "It's not a problem if it's an Issue"

Catco is a manufacturer of catalytic heaters used in the natural gas industry to prevent freezing. Founded in 1982 by Bill Richards in a small space behind a tractor dealership in Terrell, Texas, the company has grown over 40 years into a trusted supplier of flameless heating solutions.

Each time Travis Richards, owner and CEO of Catco, has rolled out an Issues List to a different department in his business, he notices the same consistent pattern. Each team starts off with surface-level concerns.

"In the beginning, what people put down as issues was usually pretty light, superficial stuff," he recalls. "I remember one of the first issues we ever put on there was, 'Should we get a foosball table for the break room?' That was seriously one of our early issues—we didn't know what we were doing yet."

But each time, he has watched as teams learn to stick with the structure provided by Level 10 Meetings and the Issue Components. They evolve and learn the right mindsets and start confronting what really moves the needle.

Each team at Catco maintains both a short-term and a long-term Issues List. "Just figuring out which bucket something belongs in—that's an art in itself," Travis said.

With experience, the team got better at working the system and using the long-term list more effectively. "Sometimes the solution is simply to say, 'We're not doing this right now,' and drop it into the 90-day list," he said.

Travis said an Issues List generates confidence that solutions can be found for any issue. "I like to say, 'It's not a problem if it's an issue.' Because once it's on the Issues List, we can deal with it."

This points to a deeper layer of the tool—the capacity to see when there is an issue. Travis sees this as a good indicator of a team member's ability to "Get it" when it comes to their role.

For example, neat work areas are a part of the culture at Catco. "If a leader walks by workstations that are a total mess and doesn't even notice, that's a Get-it problem," Travis said. "They don't see the issue as an issue—and that's where trouble starts."

In his experience, only two types of issues can truly bite a business. "One is the issue people do not have the courage to tell you about. The other is the one they don't even realize exists."

The real question for leaders is what kind of culture they're building. "If people aren't raising their hands, you've got to ask: What is it about this place that makes them stay quiet?" he said.

Once an issue makes a list, IDS is a winning formula for solving it. Travis got a reminder of how much more productive meetings are with structure when he attended an external meeting about local economic development.

"The only agenda was basically: sit around and talk about it," he said. "It was brutal." Travis had a similar experience during his time in the Air Force, where meetings often had the same problem: "The agenda was just to talk."

It's all a reminder of the drift that will happen in most meetings without a commitment to IDS. And even with Catco's commitment to it, Travis said it still takes reminders and discipline to stay on track.

"It's easy for a good company to slip from IDS into D-D-D-D—just Discuss, Discuss, Discuss, Discuss." The key is shared language. "When everyone understands that we're here to Identify, Discuss, and Solve, we can rein it back in when people start to wander."

CHAPTER 4

• • • • • • • • • • • • • •

IDS STEP 1—IDENTIFY

Time to take a breath and reorient.

Because we are about to drill down to the heart of everything.

The core of this book, yes. But also the central skill that separates great leaders and Leadership Teams from the average. The subject of this chapter is the pivot point that can permanently change the way problems, challenges, and opportunities are approached in any business. Done right, it will be a total transformation.

In his Foreword, Gino Wickman shared this remarkable observation that is worth repeating in full: *"A strong Leadership Team, after calling out all of the issues, is fanatical about resolving them. They typically solve 5 to 15 issues every week in their weekly meeting and 30 per quarter in their quarterly planning sessions, regardless of whether it's a people issue, a new idea, an opportunity, or a business problem. For strong Leadership Teams, issues never linger."*

It could be easy to skim those numbers and fail to pause and see how exceptional they are. Five to 15 a week, and 30 in one quarterly planning session—and doing that consistently! Any business that can solve that many issues that fast and permanently is in control of their destiny, as most of our clients are.

Identify-Discuss-Solve is the key, and Identify is the hardest of these to master. But the time spent honing the skills necessary will unlock everything you want from your business.

One common misstep when solving issues is to rush through (or even skip) the Identify step. Take your time here to really dig deep on identifying the root of the issue. Discuss and Solve are also worthless without Identify coming first.

Recall the "meeting hell" we described in chapter 1. The reason a typical business meeting is torture is because most companies dive right into Discuss without laying the right foundation: identifying the root first. They will discuss and discuss and discuss, but they are spinning their wheels because they skipped identifying the heart of the matter.

They spend endless amounts of time describing an issue. Or complaining about an issue. Or hiding from an issue by hopping topics when it gets too hard. These meetings are a perfect example of the classic quip: *"Meetings are where minutes are kept and hours are lost."*

It's why so many people loathe the amount of time spent in meetings, because rehashing the same old discussion is *bor-ing*. Without getting to the root first, most talk goes in circles.

THE PATH TO MASTERY

Most of the businesses we help are caught up in the epidemic of failing to solve issues fast and permanently, and lack the crucial skill of Identification in particular.

When it comes to getting to the nucleus of issues, which of these best matches your business?

- **Rookie:** You and your team struggle to stick with one issue at a time and discover the root of it.
- **Intermediate Skills:** Yours is a company in training that faithfully uses the Issues List and Issues Solving Track (IDS) to solve challenges and grab opportunities. You're not perfect, but the more you grasp how it works, the hungrier you get for true expertise. The courage to take on difficult issues grows.
- **Mastery:** The Leadership Team gets to the root of issues amazingly fast, almost effortlessly (although making this look so effortless took lots of lessons and hard work). From there, they openly and honestly execute the Discuss step, and then fearlessly Solve.

The good news is, where exactly you are right now matters less than where you commit to go. As we're about to dive deeper on the details, keep the vision of total mastery firmly in mind. **The most important step to reach your vision is becoming relentless about digging to the root of an issue, then having the courage to deal with it once you get there.** Work the Issues Solving Track, combine it with all the other EOS Tools, and don't stop. At some point, you will look up and realize you and your Leadership

Team have transformed your thinking. You're no longer the team that could not stay focused on even one topic long enough to permanently solve it; you're now the team that can do it 5 to 15 times a meeting.

PRIORITIZATION

Pick Three and Go!

This is just what it sounds like. You're not going to spend 15 minutes going around and asking everyone to vote on the priorities. Instead, say, "Okay, everybody, it's time to solve issues. Take 15 seconds, review the list, and call out our top three priorities." The idea is to jump-start the process, not spend a lot of time arguing about priority.

A natural objection to this method could be, "But what if we are not picking the 'right' ones, the issues we need to address immediately?"

There are two points to make here. First, if an issue is truly a crisis, then simply call it out as number one! If your car is in a ditch, your immediate priority is to get it out of the ditch and back on the road. If the building is on fire, you don't do anything else until you put it out. Anything that's truly urgent and important on the list becomes number one to Identify-Discuss-Solve.

Second, go ahead and take the risk that you might be solving the "wrong" issue in terms of priority. Even if you choose "wrongly," you're building the right team skills. Picking three and going is a discipline that says, "We're a passionate, prepared group, let's go!"

A bigger worry than getting the priority wrong is when everyone hangs back, afraid to call out a first, second, and third. If this happens, try these prompts to get the team moving:

Be Selfish

Surely everyone has some obstacle, friction, opportunity, or idea in their head that they want solved. They should not hold back out of deference. Tell them, "Be selfish! What do *you* want solved?"

Be Hungry

Instead of letting a list overwhelm the team, see it as a big buffet. Everyone should arrive hungry and start eating (solving issues). If you're hungry to solve things, and you have a full Issues List in front of you, the team should be attacking issue after issue and be full by the end of the meeting.

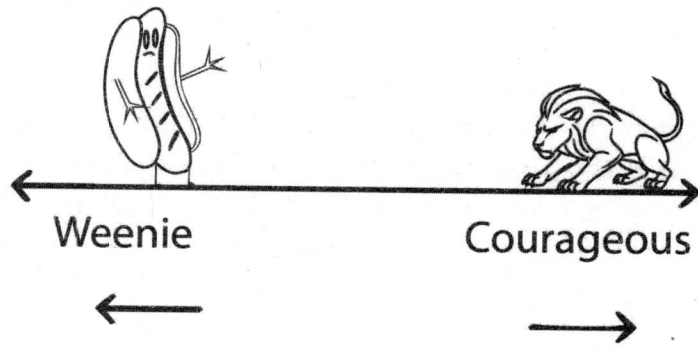

Weenie   Courageous

Worst First

What's the one issue that scares everyone to approach more than any other? What one idea or opportunity would bring the most money and results? What one issue would have the greatest impact if you solved it permanently? When in doubt on prioritizing, just ask which one is the toughest? Eat that frog.

Generally it can also be helpful to remind your leaders that this is the job they are there to do: solving the biggest issues of the company. They should not be timid or hold back.

For a concrete example of "Pick Three and Go!" in action, see the section "Running a Meeting with the Issues Solving Track."

COMPARTMENTALIZATION

All issues need to be divided into short- and long-term issues.

Sorting the Issues List into short- and long-term priorities is a key leadership tool because it will build the muscle of patience. Many leaders jump somewhat randomly from problem to problem, opportunity to opportunity, and the priorities are set by whatever is in their head at the moment.

Others just want everything solved at the same time. The lack of focus and the inability to prioritize leads to busywork, useless stress, and frustration throughout the organization.

Compartmentalizing the Issues List is a counterweight to trying to solve everything at once. It puts your challenges, opportunities, and ideas in writing and says, "Choose. Which ones need to be solved now or in the next 90 days? And which ones are important, but need to wait for now?" This helpful Compartmentalization Tool can help you give each issue a home.

1 YEAR	90-DAY	7-DAY	ISSUES	
GOALS	ROCKS	TO-DOS	LONG	SHORT
			+90 DAYS	-90 DAYS
			V/TO®	Level 10 Meeting®

A team that learns to compartmentalize will tolerate more risk on its Issues List. The stress of trying to solve five challenges at once makes everyone more risk averse. By having the patience to solve one issue at a time, the team can focus enough to reduce the obstacle to its essentials. You take smarter risks when you have a thorough grasp of the issue.

Ultimately, an Issues List gives great leaders a tool to help them prioritize strategically. It puts everything in front of you, and you can laser-focus on what has the greatest impact, balancing urgency with importance.

Don't Get Addicted to Easy

You might be tempted, when prioritizing the Issues List, to emphasize quantity over quality. It feels better to knock five easy things off the list instead of taking a deep breath and tackling that one gigantic Elephant in the Room.

If you need training wheels at the very beginning and want to focus on smaller stuff just to get everyone used to the method, that's fine. But if you stay in the shallow end for too long, you might start getting addicted to just checking things off the list. Instead, get your team hooked on solving what will move the needle the most.

We're now ready to dive deeply into identifying the root of issues.

COMMANDMENT #6 FOR SOLVING ISSUES: THOU SHALT NOT TRY TO SOLVE THEM ALL

Take issues one at a time, in order of priority. What counts is not quantity but quality. You're never going to solve them all. The faster you understand that, the better your odds are of staying calm. Solve the most important one first, then move to the next.

When doing this, you'll find some of the other issues on the list will drop off, because they were symptoms of deeper issues that you solved.

THE PURPOSE OF IDENTIFY

Simply stated, the goal of the Identify step is to uncover the cause of your symptoms at the root, rather than just treating symptoms. It's no longer, "Just make these symptoms go away." Your mindset will evolve into thinking critically and systematically.

Another way to say it comes from *Traction*: "Clearly identify the real issue, because the stated problem is rarely the real one. The underlying issue is always a few layers down." At EOS, we like to say, "Dig, dig, dig." And then, if you haven't hit bedrock, dig some more.

Running a Meeting with the Issues Solving Track

1. Choose someone to run the meeting.

2. Have the issues read aloud, then choose and prioritize the top three. Please note that you might not be perfect at prioritizing at first. Don't get hung up on this. Just do your best to prioritize correctly without endlessly agonizing about it.

3. Now take the top issue ("Take #1!") and get going, using the Who–Who–1 Sentence technique (see hereafter).

4. Stick with one issue at a time. If the team strays off track, anyone in the meeting can and should call that out by shouting something like, "Tangent Alert!" or "Squirrel!"

5. Similarly, if the group loses attention while digging to the root, the person running the meeting needs to get things refocused fast. No wandering off into aimless discussion by endlessly describing the surface of the issue. And no proposing solutions until the root is identified.

A good method for clearly defining issues in meetings is **Who–Who–1 Sentence:**

- The first *Who* is deciding who is raising the issue. (Kate says she is raising an issue in order fulfillment, so she is the first Who.)

- The second *Who* is the person accountable for solving the issue. (Dan is in charge of order fulfillment, making him the second Who.)

- The *1 Sentence* needs to come from the person raising the issue. They look the person who is accountable in the eye and state the issue in ***one sentence.*** That sentence needs to be concise, to the point, and include no cushioning or politicking. Don't start with preambles or rambling stories. Hit the nerve, rip the Band-aid off, and get right to it.

For example, Kate could say this 1 Sentence to Dan, "Order fulfillments are two weeks behind our promised delivery dates."

(For a longer example of Who–Who–1 Sentence, see chapter 7.)

WAYS TO IDENTIFY

Don't be too prescriptive when telling a team how to identify the root of an issue. Imagine dumping a puzzle out of the box onto a table and then trying to give exact piece-by-piece instructions on how to put it together. It would never work.

But what you could do is provide some puzzle-solving techniques to point strongly in the right direction, such as, "Start by putting the border pieces together," "Sort by color and pattern," and "Use a spacious table and have good lighting."

In this spirit, here are some strategies, questions, and methods to help you think through identifying the root.

QUESTIONS THAT LEAD SOMEWHERE

What outcome/result is this issue preventing us from achieving?

This question can be revealing in several directions. It may uncover the fact that the issue isn't all that important and you don't need to waste time on it. Why would you, if it's not preventing a key outcome or result?

Other times, it will spur you to connect the issue to related issues that are all blocking you from a key result. How are these symptoms connected and what (or who) do they point to?

Is this a barrier, obstacle, idea, or opportunity?

If you're stuck on how to dig down a level, ask the most basic question: What kind of "object" do we have in front of us? Obviously, this question will not get you all the way to the root in one fell swoop, but it can start you digging in the right place.

Why? Why? Why? Why? Why?

Most people are familiar with the 5 Whys technique. Originally developed by Toyota founder Sakichi Toyoda, it's well suited to getting to the root of issues. As a refresher, it works like this:

- State the problem or opportunity: Clearly define the issue you're trying to solve.
- Ask "Why?" Identify why the problem occurred or what the opportunity is.
- Ask "Why?" again. Dig deeper into the answer to the previous "Why?"
- Continue asking "Why?" as many as five times until you reach the root.

    Here's an example from a roofing company:

1. Why did we have to run supplies to our installers in the field in the middle of three different jobs last month? They were out of nails.
2. Why were they out of nails? No one checked the trucks in the morning.
3. Why did no one check the supply of such a basic item? The job supervisor did not use the morning pre-job check sheet.

4. Why did the supervisor not use the morning pre-job check sheet? We haven't printed them in forever.

5. Why are we still printing pre-job check sheets in the first place? No one ever created an electronic version for the supervisor's mobile tablet.

- **Root:** The process of the morning checklist isn't being followed because its format is out of date.

This is perhaps a bit simplified, but you get the idea. For complex, multifactor issues, it may take several more than five.

If we were courageous, how would we approach this?

This is a particularly good question if you sense the team is holding back, afraid to Enter the Danger. It has a touch of humor to take the edge off, but is still pointed enough to spur honesty.

Here's an example of courage and honesty one of us witnessed in a meeting that speaks to this idea. The Leadership Team of the company in question was deeply frustrated. They had just missed their goals for the second year in a row, and were doing a postmortem in preparation for another round of goal-setting. Nothing being said so far in the meeting was going to change their trajectory, and the Leadership Team knew it.

Tension was building because they could not accept another year of missed goals, but no progress was being made to get to the root cause of the issues. The EOS Implementer suggested another look at the Accountability Chart and put it up in front of the group. No one engaged with it much, so the Implementer called a 10-minute break.

When the group returned, the sales leader said, "I know what the answer is. No one is going to like it, and I volunteer to be the first to go. But the root problem is our company cannot support our structure. We have to downsize."

The room got still. Someone had finally said how they would deal with the issue if they had courage. Despite the fact that it would directly affect several people in the room, they revised the Accountability Chart and followed through on a necessary downsize.

The following year, they met their goals, and the company is still thriving.

What would great look like?

You can open your mind to other possibilities for solving a challenge by asking how it would look if the opposite were happening. What would it look like if you were great at whatever is now causing friction? This is another type of question that will probably not get you all the way to the root immediately, but it can put you on the right path.

COMMANDMENT #4 FOR SOLVING ISSUES: THOU SHALT NOT RELY ON SECONDHAND INFORMATION

You can't solve an issue involving multiple people without all the parties present. If the issue at hand involves more than the people in the room, schedule a time when everyone can attend. One client calls these "pow-wows." When someone brings him an issue involving others or secondhand information, he says, "Time for a pow-wow," and pulls everyone involved together and solves it.

THINKING TOOLS

Most of what we are doing in this chapter is uncovering ways to think as clearly as possible. "Questions that lead somewhere" are one way to do that. But you can take it up another notch by using mental models: a lens your brain uses to make sense of the world, solve issues, and make decisions. We are going to touch on them only briefly here, but if you want to go a little deeper, check out the Mental Models section in "Checklists, Templates, and Tools."

"WHAT ARE THE INCENTIVES?"

When you're searching for the root of anything, asking about incentives can be revealing. Money is one incentive, of course, but there are psychological and emotional incentives too.

When you get stuck, stop and ask, "What are the incentives here?"

ASSUME POSITIVE INTENT

It often feels natural, when something goes wrong, to assume that someone has knowingly acted with bad intentions.

The truth is that most people aren't trying to cause harm; breakdowns are often the result of misunderstandings and mistakes. (Formally this is often called Hanlon's Razor: the idea that most problems happen because of mistakes, ignorance, or incompetence, not because of bad intentions or conspiracies.)

Recognizing this helps us look at issues more objectively and with less bias and suspicion.

MAPPING OUT CAUSE AND EFFECT

Sometimes when you're struggling to get to the root of an issue, it can help to go a little deeper in your thinking. A lot of thought stops at the first level: focusing on what happens now.

Asking "What happens next? What ripple effects will this choice create?" and mapping out the cause and effect of decisions (second-order thinking) can help you weigh trade-offs.

EOS AS A MENTAL MODEL

EOS isn't just a system; it's a way to think differently about your business. The six components provide an integrated, holistic context for your team's actions.

Businesses running on EOS don't always notice this immediately. What they see at first is six components they need to master, and the tools that show them how to do it. They work the system and get results, and that's the exact right approach.

But over time, they also **begin to see that EOS becomes a complete lens, a mental model that cuts through the noise and zeroes in on what really matters to get what they want from their business.**

The connections between the components and how they affect each other become clearer the more they implement the system. Often they begin to see that the tools are all trying to signal the same basic issues.

If you run on EOS with openness and honesty, you begin to see that the signals are part of a larger story. When you look at a specific issue, what story is it telling you about the friction in the business? Have other tools been pointing to the same thing? And what is that thing (i.e., the root of the issue)?

To illustrate this, one of our clients purchased glasses with the EOS Model on the lenses, so they could look at their business through the lens of the Six Key Components. Consider viewing every issue through the perspective of Vision, People, Data, Issues, Process, or Traction. The root of every issue always lives in one of these six.

KNOWING WHEN YOU'VE NAILED IT

Getting to the root is both art and science. The art of it comes in knowing when you have landed on it.

At times it will be fairly obvious. In those cases, there is an "Aha!" moment and the entire team feels it. It creates an almost tangible energy on the team and makes you ready to Discuss and Solve with gusto.

Other times, getting to the root will feel like hitting bedrock. Perhaps it isn't a dramatic "That's it!" moment, but you will know you have sincerely dug as deep as possible and that no more digging will add value. Your confidence level that you have reached the root is high.

Another way you know you have nailed it is, if you're using a whiteboard or flipchart, it's the thing you want to circle and double-underline. You see it as the center of all the connections that were made on this issue.

When these things happen, you're ready to move on to Discuss and Solve.

PITFALLS

It can take some time for the team to get used to being completely honest about the people, processes, and whatever else is in front of you. If past meetings have been more like circular discussions, it can be easy to slip back into old habits.

Watch out for common mistakes and signs that you are off track. Here are some typical pitfalls with suggested fixes:

JUMPING TO CONCLUSIONS

Part of an open and honest culture is avoiding jumping to conclusions. Sometimes we don't even realize when we are jumping to a preconceived "solution." We want to be right (for both good and bad reasons), which means we sometimes overlook facts and perspectives that contradict our conclusions.

When you're heading into a meeting where IDS will be happening, make an extra effort to let go of the need to be right. Listening to others can open us up to those times when we are getting it wrong.

Particularly key in combating preconceived conclusions is data. Slow down and hear what the signals are saying. In the EOS book *Data*, you can find more guidance on using data to solve issues.

CONFUSING ACTIVITY WITH ACHIEVEMENT

This can happen in two distinct ways when IDSing. One, you can confuse talking about an issue with doing something about it. "We're talking about it, that must be progress!" Maybe it is and maybe it isn't, but nothing is accomplished until you have actually gone all the way to a Solve. Remember that Effort ≠ Results. In other words, the amount of effort you put in isn't the same as the results. Talking and talking about something might feel like effort, but it isn't getting you anywhere.

This confusion between activity and accomplishment also comes into play when analyzing an issue. Just because some issue has a lot of resources (human and otherwise) being poured into it doesn't mean the effort is effective. Look beyond busywork and ask, "What are we really doing?"

YOUR INTERNAL DIALOGUE IS LOUDER THAN YOUR EXTERNAL DIALOGUE

Have you ever been listening in a meeting and thought that everything being said was off point, wrong, or both? When that happens, you have a mismatch between the dialogue that is happening in front of you and the conversation you're having with yourself.

Your internal dialogue wants to escape and inject truth (or at least your perspective) into the situation. But something is stopping you. A misguided idea of politeness, fear of harming someone's sacred cow, or discouragement that change will never happen (so why bother?).

You keep it to yourself, and complain to your spouse about it later, telling them what you would have said. Or you find a like-minded colleague to gossip with after, to enjoy the misery a little bit.

Very simply, you are doing your team a disservice when you hold back the unfiltered conversation in your head. If you find yourself doing that, it's a sure sign that you need to speak up.

AWKWARD SILENCE

When good questions are asked but someone quickly changes the subject, or a question is sort of answered, but is then followed by an awkward silence because everyone can sense it was a dance around accountability and truth, those are red flags of avoidance.

When these silences happen, who is willing to Enter the Danger and ask the question again?

GETTING DISTRACTED BY OTHER ISSUES

As you dig for the root of an issue, it's common for additional issues to surface. This is fine, except that it will often send teams down a whole new path and the meeting will derail. If other issues come to light, simply add them to your list, and then continue to stay focused on the issue at hand.

FIGHTING FIRES INSTEAD OF PREVENTING THEM

You may be tempted to think, after you have "put out a fire" (fixed a crisis), that you have solved something. Maybe you have, but you likely still have not identified the root of the issue that caused the challenge in the first place.

Consider an actual fire department. They do solve the problem of fires by putting them out, and that's what most of us visualize first when we think of a fire department.

But fire departments spend about 90 percent of their time preventing fires or figuring out ahead of time how to minimize them. They carry out inspections and educate the public on fire safety. They also go back after a fire and investigate what happened so future fires can be prevented.

Many teams can figure out how to "put out a fire" in their business, but how many go back and investigate what happened? Too many businesses confuse putting out a fire with identifying the cause. To truly perform the Identify step, you need to ask:

- How did this fire start in the first place?
- What "inspections" should have been done to prevent it?
- Are there embers still smoldering that are going to bring back a fully raging fire?

COMMANDMENT #8 FOR SOLVING ISSUES: THOU SHALT CHOOSE SHORT-TERM PAIN AND SUFFERING

Both long-term and short-term pain involve suffering. You have a choice between the two with all of the issues you face.

If you're wrestling with a tough decision, whether it involves strategy, customers, or people, and you're procrastinating, you're choosing long-term pain. Solve your problem now rather than later. The fear of doing it is worse than actually doing it. Choose short-term suffering.

JUMPING STRAIGHT TO DISCUSS OR SOLVE

Keeping the conversation laser focused on digging for the root is challenging. It takes discipline not to chase tangents. People naturally want to vent, complain, describe, and stick to the surface, where the ground feels safer. A good meeting facilitator can step in when things get sidetracked and ask, "Is this related to the root of the issue? How? Make the connection."

Here is a simplified example of where Discuss before Identify goes wrong:

Issue: Sales are down 5 percent over last year. Why is that, and what can be done to reverse that?

The group dives in and a rambling discussion ensues. All sorts of things are thrown in the mix at the surface.

"The economy is flat, that must have a lot to do with it."

"We should get more referrals. Those close much easier." (Followed by a mishmash of ideas on how to increase referrals.)

"We just need to up our closing rate. And our sales manual is out of date. Maybe we should rewrite it. If our frontline sales team had better and more up-to-date direction, we would close more sales."

And on it goes. Finally, the boss gets fed up. They had this same meeting last month. "I thought I said to rewrite the sales manual after we talked about it last time. Let's get that done!"

No one in the meeting redirected the conversation to focus on the root of why sales are down. Is the closing rate actually down? Is it the quantity of leads? Is it the quality of the leads? Has anyone asked the salespeople whether they even look at the sales manual?

No one is digging beneath the surface to ask the next question, and then the question after that.

Here's what digging for the root of the issue could have looked like.

Recall that the issue is that sales are down 5 percent. The team is seeking to understand why, and what can be done to increase them.

"What's the close rate?"

"It is actually up a couple of percentage points. Which tells us the issue is probably not the sales manual or the process our sales team is using. It also tells us that our lead quality is probably holding steady or even a little better."

If the close rate is up and sales are down, the sales team must not be getting in front of enough prospects. Time to keep digging.

To condense this example, the team keeps digging and finds that leads from the website, Pay-Per-Click, and trade shows are all steady. But one lead source has dried up: cold-call prospects.

These calls have a stated weekly goal, but it turns out no one has tracked that in forever. This is likely at the root of the issue. The Discuss and Solve could take a few directions, but it should be an extremely focused debate now that the Identify step has hit bedrock.

If your organization is struggling with the Identify step, remembering what is at stake can snap things back to reality. You will never escape reactive mode and treating symptoms until you train yourself and your company to be fierce about the Identify step. Until then, the same old inefficiencies, busywork, and recurring issues will keep happening.

All it takes to change that is a ruthless commitment to identifying the ultimate causes of friction in your business.

. . . .

Solving Issues in Real Life

Aggressive Hydraulics: Getting Clarity Faster

Aggressive Hydraulics, founded in 2002 and based in Minnesota, specializes in designing and manufacturing purpose-built hydraulic cylinders for a variety of industries. The company is committed to American-made quality.

Aggressive Hydraulics made the decision to bring in an EOS Implementer in late 2018. Given what happened just over a year later, it turned out to be the right decision.

When COVID hit in early 2020, the structure provided by EOS proved invaluable in helping the company stay grounded during a time of great uncertainty. Aggressive Hydraulics had to remain open to support critical infrastructure projects and emergency services, but there was no playbook for how to do that.

One key to succeeding in unprecedented times was getting better at handling issues. Before working with Expert EOS Implementer Sue Hawkes, the team often spun its wheels trying to solve issues. "We'd spend a lot of time talking around a problem without ever really solving it," company president Paul Johnson explained. "And if not everyone was clear on what the issue actually was, those meetings could turn into a bit of a venting session. People might feel better in the moment, but we weren't moving forward."

The consequences of that lack of clarity around identifying the root of an issue went beyond just unproductive meetings. "When employees leave a meeting without clear action steps or a sense that we're actually addressing the root cause, it chips away at morale," Vice President of Operations Joel Tjepkes said. "If people go week after week living in the same problems with no resolution, it starts to affect culture and confidence in leadership."

That's exactly what led the team to adopt EOS and commit to a better way of handling issues. The IDS framework helped them break the cycle of endless discussion by forcing alignment on what the real issue was—before diving into solutions. "Now, we're not afraid to hit the pause button if something doesn't feel right," Joel said. "We'll take time to get the facts and ensure we are aligned on what the issue is, then come back ready to actually solve it."

Paul echoed that, describing how the Leadership Team used to jump in with solutions without fully understanding the problem.

One example was a rise in warranty claims, which initially looked like a quality control issue. "We brought in the usual voices, made a lot of assumptions, and threw fixes at what turned out to be the wrong problem," Paul said. "Eventually, we realized it was a process and training issue. EOS helped us get to that clarity faster."

Today, their meetings have structure, ownership, and follow-through. "The Level 10 format gives us a consistent space to tackle issues," Paul said. "We don't rely on drive-by 'got-a-minute' conversations anymore. Everything has a place, and every issue has an owner."

It's important to Paul and Joel that the company develops employees not just as workers, but as people who have the opportunity to grow and improve personally.

They have witnessed remarkable transformations in team members through the IDS problem-solving process. "It's been a real confidence booster for employees who previously struggled with self-doubt but now regularly solve complex problems through our team approach," Joel explains.

Seeing this development has been incredibly rewarding. "It's awesome and impactful to not only positively influence an employee at work but to see their home life improve as well," Joel said.

Paul agreed, and shared how he's seen the tools empower the team. "Our more seasoned employees have learned the IDS mindset and apply it to their Level 10 Meetings," Paul said. "Those employees also provide peer-to-peer coaching to new team members, which has been great to see. They'll offer suggestions like, 'Can you better phrase the issue?' or 'That sounds like multiple issues,' or 'Let's prioritize our issues before we jump in.'"

Paul added that it's made the team members more engaged. "It's also helped our employees be more part of the solution. Previously, they may have felt addressing issues and opportunities was someone else's job—now, they understand it takes all of us and feel comfortable bringing issues up and tackling them," he said. "In one of our Engineering L10s we had a new team member bring up an issue regarding fixturing for a product in manufacturing. This brought awareness to the larger issue that we didn't have a single point of accountability for Manufacturing Engineering. This was impactful because that new team member set the example of calling out issues and stepping up to solve them, as well as helping us identify a larger accountability issue that our Leadership Team needed to be aware of."

Reflecting on the EOS journey, Joel said, "Looking back on when we started versus now, we're much stronger for having gone through it. We've learned not just how to fix problems, but how to understand them. That's what really changed things for us—and for the culture too."

CHAPTER 5

. . . .

IDS STEP 2—DISCUSS

If you and your team have carried out the Identify step well, you're now set up for an exceptionally productive discussion. But danger lurks. For many teams entering the Discuss step, the temptation to lose focus is huge.

To help you avoid this fate, this chapter is constructed to be just like your discussion should be: laser focused and to the point.

We will not be too prescriptive in telling you exactly how to discuss an issue—that would be counterproductive and impossible. Instead, we will give you nine guidelines to make discussions fruitful and high performing. Then we will share some additional thoughts and warnings of what to avoid.

NINE GUIDELINES TO IDS LIKE A PRO

1. Everyone has to have some level of input. Go around the table and have each person speak, even if what they want to say is, "I have no opinion."

2. Don't pile on. Don't repeat what you already said. **Saying it once is essential, saying it twice or more is just politicking.**

3. You must stay focused on solving this issue. You can't skip around to other issues. If someone is getting off track, call back to the root. "*This is what we're discussing. Let's make sure it's related as directly as possible to solving THIS.*" Put the issue and the root of it up on the board and point at it if that helps.

4. A meeting runner should be identified to keep things focused. Ideally, this would be someone committed to (and good at) keeping the discussion concise and fixated on the issue at hand.

5. Open and Honest is just as essential here as it was during the Identify step. This is actually where Enter the Danger sometimes becomes even more challenging. Saying the idea out loud can feel scary depending on the issue.

6. Don't shame people for ideas, proposals, and attempts at a solution. Everyone should feel empowered to speak from their perspective and encouraged even if their solution is not adopted. In other words, everyone should feel like they can "take a shot" at it (see Commandment #10 hereafter).

7. You know it's time to bring discussion to a close when things are getting redundant. It might be helpful to think of this as the Zipper Rule. Has it been said already by

someone else? Then don't say the same thing all over again; just say that you agree and then zipper the lips!

8. Everyone needs to agree that after the discussion, they are done with it forever. **It's time to commit.** No meetings after the meeting. If you aren't ready to commit, you have to voice disagreements now, in the moment. A team that trusts each other doesn't play politics. Even if it's not the decision you would make, if you've voiced all your disagreements and the decision didn't go your way, you need to disagree and commit.

9. The discussion is *not* about getting a decision by consensus. You can't run a company like that. There must be a decision by the appropriate person, not a vote. Usually it will be the leader of the team, but when an issue has been brought by a particular team member that needs help, they can say whether it is solved. For those that run on EOS, the tie breaker on the Leadership Team will be the Integrator.

It's important to note that about 80 or 90 percent of the time, the solution will be clear and the leader's decision widely acknowledged. For the 10 to 20 percent where there needs to be a more controversial decision at the end of the discussion, the Integrator must make the call.

COMMANDMENT #10 FOR SOLVING ISSUES: THOU SHALT TAKE A SHOT

Taking a shot means that you should propose a solution. Don't wait around for someone else to solve it. If you're wrong, your team will let you know. Sometimes the discussion can drag on because everyone is afraid to voice a solution even though someone may have it right on the tip of his or her tongue. Don't be afraid to take a shot. Yours might be the good idea.

"SQUIRREL!"

A great resource for helping everyone in your organization understand EOS better is *What the Heck Is EOS?* by Gino Wickman and Tom Bouwer. This book is written specifically for employees of companies running on EOS. Here is a short excerpt that explains how to handle things when the team loses focus on the issue at hand:

> You don't have to sit there helplessly [when the team gets off topic]. When this starts to happen, do what we teach every client. Simply say, "Tangent Alert!" This is a great way to alert your team to the fact that the conversation has started to go sideways and needs to be brought back to the original issue.

> Another way to illustrate this is just to call out "Squirrel!" when the team starts darting off in a random direction. Everyone seems to get this image immediately. It's a great way to stop unfocused discussions in a humorous but effective way.

Remember that "the road is paved with squirrels that couldn't decide." Stay on task! (And for more on using animals as illustrations and reminders, see chapter 8.)

COMMANDMENT #3 FOR SOLVING ISSUES: THOU SHALT BE DECISIVE

In the classic book *Think and Grow Rich*, Napoleon Hill cited a study that analyzed 25,000 people who had experienced failure. Lack of decision, or procrastination, was one of the major causes. In contrast, analysis of several hundred millionaires revealed that every one of them had the habit of reaching decisions promptly and changing them slowly. It's less important what you decide than it is that you decide ... so, decide!

THREE PATHS

Sometimes teams find themselves in a discussion of an issue they are actually hesitant to solve. They identify the root of it, then realize the solution is going to require the sacrifice of a sacred cow.

When you have a particularly difficult impurity or obstacle to discuss, it can be helpful to ask this about the issue: Are you going to live with this issue, end this issue, or change this issue? Because those are literally the *only* three options.

If discussion is stalled because you're afraid to confront these options, you need to ask a follow-up question, because if you can no longer live with it, you have to end it or change it, and that will require decisive action:

What are the circumstances under which you might live with something that is hurting your business?

Only you can answer that, but we have seen cases where someone simply will not make a People Component decision because they think the implications are too messy. Our recommendation is to always do what is best for the Greater Good, but some still choose to live with what is hurting them.

If you do decide to live with it, have your eyes wide open and . . .

- Don't complain about it ever again.
- Don't put it on the Issues List ever again, because it will just waste everyone's time.
- Be honest with yourself that *at best* you will have to grow in spite of it—and that may be a much longer trip.

- Also, own the fact that living with it could have significant consequences for your business and the people who work inside it.

Essentially you are saying, "I'm willing to commit to living with it, I understand what it means, and I am willing to face those facts. I am going to shut up about it forever and never whine about it again."

But let's say that you have decided you will end it or change it. That means it's time to go all in on an authentic discussion.

You might be pleasantly surprised to find there is a total vibe shift compared to previous meeting discussions. The groundwork of identifying the root of the issue makes all the difference. Now the discussion can be about something real, and free from tangents.

The main focus of the discussion should be this: What's the best solution for the Greater Good? What you are truly aiming for are suggestions for the best way to solve this issue. During the Solve step, you will then refine it and add specific action steps.

COMMANDMENT #7 FOR SOLVING ISSUES: THOU SHALT LIVE WITH IT, END IT, OR CHANGE IT

This is a great lesson Gino Wickman learned from his dad, a very successful entrepreneur. In solving an issue, he teaches that you have three options: You can live with it, end it, or change it. There are no other choices. With this understanding, you must decide which of the three it's going to be. If you can no longer live with the issue, you

have two options: Change it or end it. If you don't have
the wherewithal to do those, then agree to live with it and
stop complaining. Living with it, however, should be the
last resort.

A FINAL THOUGHT FOR THE DISCUSS STEP

As your team's discussion moves forward, it can be helpful to remember this concept: The simplest explanation or solution is usually the best one.

(This way of thinking is often referred to as Occam's Razor, but what you call it isn't important. What matters is that you use the principle.)

This isn't about oversimplifying or cutting corners. It's about clarity. It's about asking, "What's the most clear-cut way to solve this?" Instead of chasing complexity, you focus on what makes the most straightforward sense.

Of course, there is no guarantee that this approach will produce the best solution every time. But this "thinking lens" holds true more often than not, and it's a great mental model to go to first when discussing the best solution.

. . . .

Solving Issues in Real Life

AccountingDepartment.com: Having the G.R.I.T. to IDS and then Commit

AccountingDepartment.com provides outsourced bookkeeping, controller, and CFO support and advisory services. Founded in 2004, the company has grown to become one of the largest and most experienced firms in its field.

Dennis Najjar, CPA, and Bill Gerber launched AccountingDepartment.com more than two decades ago with a plan for continual growth, something they have pursued with great intention.

In 2018, the company attempted to self-implement EOS. While they made some progress and adopted various components, it never fully came together as a cohesive system. So in 2023, they decided to hire an EOS Implementer to guide continued growth and ensure the long-term health of the company.

Before EOS, HR Director Lisa Archetti said the organization operated in silos: "Prior to EOS, we all met with the co-founders at a department level individually. I had to present an agenda every week before we met." This siloed approach created significant alignment problems because, as Lisa put it, "We would solve things in those meetings, but not always understand the effect that it would have on another department because that perspective wasn't represented."

Implementation Director Nancy Gordon agrees, adding that a regular weekly meeting of the entire Leadership Team transformed their collaborative process dramatically.

"It brought all the leaders of each department together and collaborating together," Nancy explains. "It created so much efficiency because everything is discussed in those meetings, and we're no longer operating in silos." Their shared Issues List ensures that when something important comes up, they "put it on the leadership issue list so it doesn't get forgotten and nothing falls through the cracks."

Another transformation was in the discussion part of meetings. Before implementing EOS, the team was great at going on and on. "We were really good at beating dead horses," is how Operations Director Amy Harold put it.

"We went in circles a lot. Dennis and Bill always wanted everyone to feel heard and represented, which is of course good, and we still want that," Amy continued. "But we needed a way to still move forward when we couldn't reach complete consensus."

The introduction of IDS put a stop to endless discussion.

"We've become so much more efficient at making decisions," Amy said. "Everyone has the chance to be heard, but we're also comfortable saying we've discussed this enough and need to make a decision to move on."

One of the most impactful lessons came early from their Implementer, who taught them about "disagree and commit" with this example:

"I may want yellow walls, Nancy may want green, and Lisa may want blue, but once we decide on blue, we all leave the meeting loving blue walls," Amy recalls. This principle of collectively owning decisions regardless of personal preferences has profoundly changed how the team resolves issues and moves forward together.

The team unanimously considers developing their Core Values through the EOS process as their favorite issue they've ever solved. "When we met and solved that, it sticks out in all our minds as the best meeting we ever had," Amy says.

When they first tried to come up with a well-defined set of Core Values, they could not all agree and land on something that completely captured it. They ran out of time on that first attempt, so their Implementer told them to put it on the Issues List and keep working it using IDS.

Amy explained why it was difficult: "We didn't want to put something down on paper that were just words. As Bill said, 'We don't want to just ChatGPT our Core Values.' If we're going to put something down that defines us, we want it defined in a way that we really are."

Nancy said it felt a little strange and frustrating that they couldn't get it right at first. "We felt like we know what we mean. Why can't we just spit it out?"

Their dedication to finding authentic Core Values that truly represented the company led to multiple meetings and brainstorming sessions. Lisa recalls, "We just didn't give up. We stuck with it in bulldog fashion until we had this moment where everyone was like, *that's it!*" This persistence reflected the very values they were trying to define—demonstrating their grit before it became the acronym of their Core Values.

The solution was created "G.R.I.T."—standing for Gratitude, Resilience, Integrity, and Teamwork. "Family First" is also a Core Value, one that has defined AccountingDepartment.com from its founding.

Nancy describes the breakthrough: "We had one of my very favorite brainstorming sessions ever, and then when we hit a note that we all felt—that's it."

Lisa adds, "The funniest part is that we wrapped it up minutes after it came out of our mouths. It took time to get there, but once we got it, we knew we nailed it, and the rest is history."

These carefully crafted Core Values quickly became embedded in every aspect of their business operations. They revamped their interview questions, job descriptions, and recognition programs around these Core Values.

"It's not just a one-time memo we send out to employees or a little snippet in the handbook. It's baked into everything we do," Lisa said.

Amy sums it up: "It's created a world of difference. There's so much pride that goes into those Core Values because they really embody who we are and paint such a whole picture of us."

CHAPTER 6

· · · · · · · · · · · · · · ·

IDS STEP 3—SOLVE

The root of the issue has been identified. An open and honest discussion followed. All the options we can think of are on the table.

Now what?

LAND. THE. PLANE.

Conclude. Conclude. Conclude.

Everything from here forward should be focused on a solution that includes specific actions and follow-up. Once you reach the Solve step, the only reason your lips should be moving is to solve the issue.

We are emphasizing the need for a decisive and clear solution because it's exactly here where so many teams trip and face-plant a few feet from the finish line.

Why do they stumble? Because the Solve steps are going to make this real.

Up to now, it's been talk. That talk has sometimes been difficult, challenging work, for sure. But still, up until this moment, it had a hypothetical quality.

When the ideas were flowing, the energy in the room could carry you forward. Digging deeper was fueling everyone. Hitting the root of an issue springs the release button and energy pours into the discussion. The momentum carries you to the decision point.

This is where the shift happens.

Now, it's no longer just ideas. You're talking about execution. Concrete steps. Precisely defined, nitty-gritty actions that you will carry out to make real change.

Execution means action, accountability, and commitment. Sometimes that's exciting, and you go full speed ahead. But not always. If the Solve is going to be hard or messy, that finish line can look kind of scary.

Nothing should be considered solved until a person (or multiple people) has a clear "to-do" that they are accountable for, or a cascading message has been clearly articulated and committed to by all (see more on this later).

The Solve might involve some short-term pain that looks like this:

- We need to completely restructure how our sales team is compensated. We know the initial upset this is going to cause, and that will cause some short-term pain.
- The person who has been with the company for 15+ years is in a leadership position, and is the owner's brother-in-law, doesn't have the capacity for his seat. He needs to be let go.
- We have to "fire" some long-term clients because the services we provide them are no longer part of our core offerings

and they are less profitable. Still, it feels kind of scary to say goodbye to that revenue. Plus, those are not going to be fun conversations with the soon-to-be ex-clients.

As you design specific action steps to carry out these kinds of decisions, you can probably imagine wanting to run and hide. These situations require a little tough love. When we're helping a business and they backpedal at this key point, we tell them very simply, "IDS can't fix what you are not willing to do."

COMMANDMENT #2 FOR SOLVING ISSUES: THOU SHALT NOT BE A WEENIE

The solution is often simple. It's just not always easy. You must have a strong will, firm resolve, and the willingness to make the tough decision.

WHEN THE GOING GETS TOUGH, REMEMBER YOUR VISION

If you are wavering because a solution is pushing you into new territory, it can be good to take a breath and reflect on what is really going on.

Part of it is simply short-term pain. (Remember Commandment #8: Thou Shalt Choose Short-Term Pain and Suffering.) It's hard to force yourself to voluntarily take on the suffering to enact a difficult Solve.

Some of it is the fear that comes with pushing into that new territory. Going there unleashes future rewards, but it doesn't feel like that at first. It just feels like disorientation. All the comforting landmarks are in the rear-view mirror.

The freshness and adventure of new territory will give you positive momentum before you know it, but you've got to put up with going through the tunnel of short-term pain.

Here is some courage for the trip.

We've worked with tens of thousands of businesses, so we have a bird's-eye view of what works and what doesn't. Teams willing to Enter the Danger and follow through with action are the ones living out amazing visions. They are the ones accomplishing things like doubling growth. They are the ones that are no longer feeling "stuck" in their business.

They are also the ones that can get even more courageous the next time because they know how excellent it feels to free themselves from friction. It's like they are earning compound interest on their courage.

The teams that can't do this stay miserable. They can't give up the thought of greatness, but they also fail to muster the courage to solve the tough issues keeping them from that greatness. They stay forever in a muddle of mediocrity.

What path will you choose?

RIGHT NOW

One of our clients, Brian Brown from Ingredient, once said:

"The right time to do the right thing is right now."

Memorably put, and we could not agree more.

SOLVE ON A VERY PRACTICAL LEVEL

A true Solve involves these four elements: time, accountability, clarity, and commitment.

TIME

Every effective and permanent solution has an element of time. When people agree to an action as part of the Solve, **there always needs to be a crystal-clear deadline attached to it.**

You also need to be conscious that some solutions will have short-term and long-term aspects. If you have let things get to a crisis on an issue, you may need to have an immediate fix to escape the crisis.

You can think of short-term versus long-term solutions in this way: If you drove your car into a ditch, the short-term solution would be to get it out of the ditch and get safely back on the road. The long-term solution would be to figure out how you got in the ditch in the first place and to make sure you never end up in another one.

You may have a similar situation in your business. If you have a crisis, solve it and "get back on the road." Then consider what the time element is on finding a long-term solution to avoid ever driving into another ditch again.

If you aren't being specific about time and deadlines, you don't have a real Solve.

Here's a great way to look at your issues in terms of priority, adapted from Steven Covey's Four Quadrants of Time Management.

Q1: Urgent & Important	**Q2: Not Urgent & Important**
Fires, crises, deadline-driven tasks	*Prevention, capability building, strategic moves*
"Server is down," "Payroll file didn't transmit," "Key client threatening to cancel."	*"Revamp onboarding process," "Replace 20-year-old ERP," "Develop second-in-command."*
Identify fast, **Discuss** only enough to ensure the root isn't missed, assign an *immediate* To-Do. When the fire is out, schedule a Q2 follow-up to keep it from returning.	Make these the *first* items you IDS every week. A solved Q2 issue eliminates dozens of future Q1 fires. Attach crisp deadlines and owners so momentum is visible.
Q3: Urgent & Not Important	**Q4: Not Urgent & Not Important**
Interruptions, noise that feels urgent	*Time wasters*
"Marketing wants a new logo by Friday," "Random report request from HQ," "Sales rep can't find the new slide deck."	*"Should we buy swag for the holiday party?" "Change the coffee brand in the kitchen?"*
Push back or delegate outside the Level 10. If it truly matters, elevate it to Q1 or Q2. Otherwise, don't let it steal precious IDS minutes.	Delete. If someone cares deeply, let them own it offline. Q4 items never belong on the Issues List.

ACCOUNTABILITY

Time is an important part of accountability, but it is not sufficient. The other key parts are who and what? Who is responsible and what exactly for? How will we confirm that it is done? What will be the consequences if it isn't done?

This should be translated into your company's system for getting things done. If you run on EOS, this will mean things like someone taking a to-do or committing to a Rock for the next 90 days. Or if significant enough, it could be set as a goal for next year. **It is absolutely crucial that clear, specific to-dos be assigned, and then followed up on in the next meeting.** You can think of this as turning a to-do into a "ta-done!"

ROCKS

In EOS, Rocks are 90-day priorities. These are the three to seven most important objectives that need to be accomplished, and each team member has their own. Living in a 90-Day World is a way to break up annual goals into manageable pieces.

CLARITY

As you finalize a solution, be ruthless about removing any vagueness. Confusion sabotages solutions. Most of the time it will be unintentional, but any kind of wiggle room can create a lack of accountability.

Take enough time to make sure every moving part of the solution is clear.

Precision is especially important if the solution involves a rollout. When cascading a message throughout the company or a department, *everyone* should agree on *every* word.

Not only that, but you should agree on the channel of communication. Spend some time thinking and talking through whether video, email, in-person chat, shared online document, instant message channel, or some other format is most appropriate. Precision in the details matters.

A helpful resource for this topic is *The Four Obsessions of an Extraordinary Executive* by Patrick Lencioni. It outlines four key disciplines that effective leaders must embrace to build and sustain healthy organizations. Presented through a leadership fable, the book follows a fictional CEO who prioritizes organizational health over short-term results, showing how clarity and consistency can drive long-term success.

To cascade messages throughout your organization, the second and third obsessions are particularly helpful. Lencioni recommends getting obsessed with organizational clarity and then overcommunicating that clarity so everyone understands and reinforces it throughout the company.

At EOS, we use the image of putting a neat, tidy bow on the solution, indicating the complete clarity your messages should have. And once that neat, tidy bow is crafted, everyone needs to get behind that message and the way it is expressed. That's what great teams do.

COMMANDMENT #1 FOR SOLVING ISSUES: THOU SHALT NOT RULE BY CONSENSUS

On a healthy team, where the vision is clear and everyone is on the same page, eight out of ten times, everyone will agree with the solution to a problem. However, sometimes they won't, and someone needs to make the final decision. That someone is the leader. Consensus management doesn't work, period. Eventually, group-consensus decisions will put you out of business. When the leader makes the final decision in these situations, not everyone will be pleased, but as long as their voices have been heard and the team is healthy, they can usually live with it. From there, you must always present a united front moving forward.

COMMITMENT

We see some teams struggle with finishing IDS strong. EOS Implementer Sean Rosensteel has labeled this "IDSD" (as in "Identify-Discuss-Solve-Discuss"). In these cases, teams go through IDS, and commit to a Solve . . . and then they go back and keep discussing it!

Often what happens is that someone will want to talk about all the other reasons this solution is great. Or they will want to discuss every detail of the "how" of the Solve and want to give more input, even after a clear solution has been committed to and a to-do has been assigned. We call this a pile-on when you should be moving on.

Don't IDSD. Continuing to dwell on what has just been solved steals time from the next issue. Great teams move on to tackle another idea, opportunity, or challenge.

Note here that at times, the Discussion and Solve steps will sometimes uncover more about the issue than was uncovered originally in the Identify step. In these cases, returning to the Identify step is justifiable in light of the new information. But recognize that you're returning to *identifying* the issue, and make sure you have a legitimate reason for doing so. Don't do it just to avoid the clarity and accountability of committing to a Solve.

If someone on the team is struggling to commit to the solution, don't paper over it. Maybe they are seeing something others don't. Fully explore it before asking for a total commitment. But understand that the final step is for everyone to be aligned and commit to the Solve. This doesn't mean everyone agrees with the decision, but it does mean that everyone agrees to be the kind of team player that gets behind a decision honestly reached. People might disagree with the solution, but as members of the team, they still agree to get completely behind the decision once it's made. You can disagree but still commit.

The time for disagreement was during the Discuss step, which is why you made sure everyone had their say then. The person in charge of the decision is responsible for listening to everyone, but he or she isn't tallying votes.

Once the decision is made, everyone commits. Don't revisit it again. No complaining or politicking. If the leader senses that team members still have reservations about committing, they need to look them in the eye and ask, "Can you live with it?"

ACTION OR AWARENESS OR RESEARCH

The book *Traction* breaks down Solves into three types:

The first is when an issue is solved and requires action. For instance, "John is going to revise the accounts receivable past-due letter to include new language." In this case, John takes the action item and completes it, and it is solved. The second is when the issue is merely awareness, and the conclusion is that everyone concurs with that awareness. For instance, "Okay, so we all agree that meetings will start on time." The third is when the issue needs more research or facts. In this case someone is assigned an action item to do the research and bring it to a subsequent meeting. For example, "Bill will gather the client data for the last two years, and we will make the issue a top priority at next week's meeting."

NOT READY TO SOLVE

There may be scenarios where you can't Solve an issue, at least not at the moment. You don't lack the will to do it; rather, you lack the capacity. A couple of examples:

- The solution may require a role that nobody on the present team is capable of fulfilling.
- You might not have other, necessary resources for it yet and will need to solve other issues to free them up.

In some cases, this will mean adding it to a long-term Issues List (on the V/TO for those companies running on EOS).

Chunking up solutions into bite-sized pieces can be an option. Solving an issue in multiple stages over time takes discipline, but good organizations do it. Just make sure you are not breaking the solution into parts to avoid a difficult action. Only do it when it's truly necessary.

BEING TRULY "SOLVED"

It's worth recapping the keys to a **true solution** to an issue:

- At least one person will have at least one very clearly defined to-do. (Sometimes there will be multiple people and multiple to-dos.) This is key to transforming from IDS into concrete action.
- The to-do should be accomplished within seven days so it can be reported as "done" at next week's meeting. Great teams know they need to get at least 90 percent of their to-dos done each week or they'll never reach their goals. It's the consistency over time that is so important. Getting things done on time adds catalyzing energy to the entire organization.
- Once you have a to-do, take the issue off the Issues List. Remember that a to-do is the issue transformed into an action. Some teams worry that it will be missed and want to keep it on the list until the to-do is completed. Take it off the list; if the to-do doesn't solve the issue at the root, we promise it will find its way back on the list.

- Messages that need to cascade throughout the company need to be worked on until they provide perfect clarity and are understood by all. Additionally, everyone needs to be crystal clear on how the message will be delivered (what format) and when. A Solve that involves messaging isn't done until this step is completed.

- Following up on all to-dos at the next meeting is absolutely crucial for this to work. If a person doesn't get theirs done, figure out what is happening. If they are truly over capacity, the person needs to have the honesty and courage to say so.

THE IMPORTANCE OF MEETING CONSISTENCY

To make any progress, teams have to be consistent on when they meet and how they do it.

Meetings of the Leadership Teams should be on the same day every week, and always at the same time. The structure of the agenda should always be the same too. Meetings should always start on time and always end on time. There should only be two legitimate excuses for anyone on the team to miss the meeting: vacation or death.

Companies that run on EOS have meetings 90 minutes in length, with the following agenda:

- Five minutes each for Segue, Scorecard, Rock Review, Customer/Employee Headlines, and the To-Do List.

- Then you spend a full 60 minutes IDSing issues.
  You read that right. Nothing else gets more than 5
  minutes, and IDS gets an hour. That's how central it is
  to EOS and your success.
- Spend 5 minutes Concluding the meeting.

If you want to be great at IDS, we urge you to make
a similar commitment. The disciplined framework you
build around the tools is just as important as the tools
themselves.

IDS—PUTTING IT ALL TOGETHER

As your team works to become great at Identify-Discuss-Solve, consistency and discipline are critical.

For example, here is one habit to develop: Don't spend too much time patting yourself on the back after one Solve in a meeting. (Of course, do celebrate if your team is just getting its bearings using this process. That's something to build on.)

Recall how many issues a great Leadership Team typically solves in one weekly meeting: 5 to 15 on average. That means they are all business when it comes to IDSing continually.

"That issue is solved then. Which one is next?" That's the mindset you need to build. It is always about momentum when it's time to IDS.

. . . .

Solving Issues in Real Life

LSR Multifamily: Solved—from Burnout to "I'm Not Sure I'll Ever Retire"

LSR Multifamily is a Texas-based company that specializes in roofing, welding, and construction services primarily for the multifamily property industry in the Dallas–Fort Worth area.

Bill Chinners had reached his breaking point. After founding LSR Multifamily in 1992 and building it for over two decades, he found himself overwhelmed with responsibilities.

With 45–50 direct reports, he couldn't enjoy a single dinner without interruptions from texts or calls. Working 60–80 hours weekly, he was searching for a way out.

"I was looking for my exit strategy," Bill recalled. "I was trying to figure out how I could exit with enough money to retire because I have no life."

Reading *Traction* in 2014 was a big discovery for Bill. "I remember thinking, 'Hey, this is exactly what we need.'" He scheduled a 90-minute meeting with EOS Implementer Jill Young, and the transformation began.

One of the most powerful tools Bill implemented was the Issues List, something he has extended throughout the organization. "Every person in our company has access to an Issues List."

Belinda Soto is the chief operating officer and Integrator at LSR. Having joined the company after it implemented EOS, she said it was the clear structure and systems that convinced her this was the right move.

"When Bill introduced me to EOS and spelled out how they operated and introduced me to their vision, it really sold me on the potential still ahead for the company," she said. "When you take a structure like EOS and the intentionality behind it, and then you take a company like LSR, it's like marrying the best of the best."

Belinda also emphasized the value of the Issues List and Issues Solving Track for more than just overcoming problems. "One of the things we also lean in on is communicating that issues are also opportunities. We're not just capturing the fires we put out."

The IDS process transformed their leadership meetings. Bill and Belinda became skilled at focusing the team on the most important issues. "Belinda always tries to lead us toward tackling the biggest issues. What's the priority, what's going to move the needle?" Bill said.

During IDS sessions, Bill insists on complete alignment before moving forward—"solve" needs to mean truly solved. "We're not going to call it solved unless there's a hundred percent buy-in from everybody in the room. 'Are you going to a hundred percent support it?' We want full arms reaching out."

For Bill, the Issues Component also became a pathway to sort the good ideas from the not-so-good. As a Visionary, he generates numerous ideas daily. "I'll probably come up with 10 to 20 a day. Most of them are bad, but every once in a while, maybe one a day is a good idea," he said. When he brings good ideas to Belinda, they use the Issues List and IDS process to transform them from concepts to intellectual property—the implemented processes that bring value to the business.

The transformation of the company went beyond business metrics to profoundly impact Bill's life. Ten years after implementing EOS, Bill's perspective has completely reversed. "Now the honest truth is that I may do this forever. I may not ever retire because I've gained so much freedom in my life through having an operating process," he shared. "I've got one direct report, my Integrator. She's got three direct reports."

There's no need to escape that kind of structure. As Bill put it, "The difference between draining me and giving me life is having the collaboration and the whole structure of EOS and our business."

CHAPTER 7

· · · · · · · · · · · · · ·

IDS EVERYWHERE

In his classic book, *Good to Great*, Jim Collins referred to a leadership style he called the "genius with a thousand helpers."

It describes an organization where the leader is a talented and visionary individual ("the genius"), but the entire system is dependent on this person's intellect, decision-making, and drive. The "helpers" in this scenario are employees or team members who execute the leader's vision without contributing meaningfully to the strategic direction of the company.

This style of management is ultimately unsustainable, particularly if you want to grow to be anything more than a run-of-the-mill company. There is no empowerment in this model for anyone except the "genius."

One leader, or even a couple of them, isn't enough if your goal is to be great. You have to empower others. The mark of a leader is they grow leaders. In fact, we like to say:

You're not a leader until you produce a leader who produces a leader.

(To give credit where it is due, this is a statement first attributed to Dr. Stephen Brown, managing director and founder of the Brown Collective.)

This quote goes to the heart of the matter. You need to spread leadership thinking and mindsets so deep in your organization that it grows a leadership pipeline. Then you'll have something.

How is it done?

If you want to teach people to think like leaders, then show them the tools leaders use to think. That's exactly why you want to grow the IDS mindset throughout your organization.

One place to start if you are the Visionary (usually the CEO and/or founder) of your company is to ask yourself if you are able to sit back and watch your team successfully solve issues about 80 percent of the time without your input.

If you are dominating every conversation, the math isn't adding up. Let's say your Leadership Team is made up of five people (including you). If you are contributing more than 20 percent of the input, there isn't an even exchange of dialogue during IDS.

This implies either that you don't trust your team, or that you don't have the Right People in the Right Seats, or that you have created the conditions and habits where people aren't comfortable challenging you. Leaders will never grow inside your business if you don't change this dynamic.

PROJECT ARISTOTLE

Project Aristotle was an effort by Google to uncover what makes a team effective. After studying more than 180 teams, they found that team success wasn't about who was on the team, but how the team interacted. The key factor? Psychological safety—the sense that team members could speak up, take risks, and be vulnerable without fear.

Google identified five traits of high-performing teams:

- Psychological Safety
- Dependability
- Structure & Clarity
- Meaning
- Impact

These findings reframed leadership around trust, openness, and shared purpose—not just talent. This should provide motivation for building a true team, not remaining stuck in the "genius with a thousand helpers" paradigm.

TRAINING FOR DEPENDENCE OR LEADERSHIP?

The blunt truth is, when you don't train your people to solve issues, you are training them to be dependent, unthinking, and intellectually lazy. We're not saying that is your intent, but it is the outcome. This is an either/or situation. Either you are growing your people or you are weakening them. There is no third direction.

This is one of the reasons why we put so much emphasis on openness, honesty, and healthy conflict in chapter 2. When everyone understands that the expectation is to contribute to the Greater Good, and that the way to do that is to bring their best selves and best ideas to the organization, the buy-in goes up. Intensity and caring increase, which in turn makes everyone more willing to engage fully whether they agree or not, while listening and learning from others.

To some this might sound like we are advocating chaos through too much input. Not at all. There are still defined teams. You are not inviting the entire organization to the Leadership Team meeting. The salespeople are not attending the operations department meeting. There is still clearly defined structure.

No matter where someone is on the Accountability Chart, everyone in the organization should have access to their team's Issues List and be taught how to IDS. Weekly departmental team meetings need to be run just like the weekly Leadership Team meeting. The bulk of the time should be spent on issues, using the same pattern of digging to the root before discussing and solving.

Each team that meets regularly needs to have its own Issues List. A common obstacle at the departmental level is that no one is regularly populating the Issues List—a sure sign that the focus and emphasis on the Issues Component isn't where it needs to be.

The first step toward removing obstacles is that the leader of the department needs to make it a focus and emphasis. The person in that seat needs to be accountable. What are they doing during the IDS portion of their weekly meeting if they don't have a list of issues?

Here are two other ideas to get things flowing:

- Give a fun award each week to whoever puts the biggest concern, idea, or admission of failure on the Issues List. By recognizing those who are fully engaged, you are also setting the tone that your culture values honesty and transparency.
- The "Take Two Quiet Minutes" exercise. This is just what it says. Give everyone two minutes of silence to write down issues that come to mind. Ideally, you would like people to put in more thought than this before the meeting, but this could get the habit going.

A TRAINING METHOD

One classic way to teach someone something new is called See One, Do One, Teach One. It can work, but sometimes it's a bit too condensed to be completely effective. Here's an update that works even better:

- I Do One, You Watch
- I Do One, You Help
- You Do One, I Help
- You Do One, I Watch

ISSUES LIST "BONUS" BENEFIT

When you get Issues Lists populated throughout the organization, it tends to have the effect of tamping down complaints, thoughtless ideas, and vague suggestions.

You might think that it would increase those, because now everyone has a chance to put whatever random complaint they have in front of a group. But here is what happens in practice.

Say someone is complaining, venting, or gossiping. Whether they are talking to a colleague or their boss, the response needs to be, "Have you put that on the Issues List? If not, you need to stop complaining/gossiping about it."

Then one of three things will happen:

- They will *not* put it on the list because they have to confront that they haven't really thought it through and don't want to take public ownership of it.
- They will put it on the list, and it will become clear during IDS that it isn't really an issue. This will usually make them think more rigorously before putting on an issue in the future.
- They will put it on the list, and it will turn out to be an issue that needs solving.

Basically, the Issues List combined with IDS is a great way to separate the wheat from the chaff. It kills bad

> behavior and keeps the conversational energy of the company focused on what matters.

THE EFFICIENCY OF IDSing VERSUS BOTTLENECKS

IDS will also be a great asset for efficient training and learning. Without a structured system, an issue that impacts the whole department is solved individual by individual (if it is solved at all).

For example, a salesperson comes to the head of sales with an opportunity or new idea. Together, they solve it.

In an ideal world, the sales leader might recognize the benefit of blasting this out to the team. But in ordinary circumstances, people get busy and distracted, and it gets overlooked.

A month later, a different salesperson comes to the leader with a similar opportunity. Again, they work through it. And so it goes: The opportunity isn't shared collectively, and so it is repeated one-on-one.

It's great that things are getting solved, but not so great that the leader is handling each situation case by case while no one else on the team is realizing the benefit of this training and learning.

Department leaders need to get their team in the habit of calling out issues for the entire team by populating the Issues List. When the group solves issues together, they cross-pollinate more learnings, improve more efficiently, and form fewer dependency-driven relationships with the one leader.

This is why we like to say that bottlenecks are always at the top of the bottle (the leadership level). If the person sitting in the operations seat on the Leadership Team isn't training their team on how to IDS and how to think, by default they are teaching everyone that the leader is the answer person. Everything has to go through them, which creates bottlenecks and friction.

In most cases, these leaders aren't trying to keep all the power for themselves consciously. They don't even like the burden. But they aren't raising leaders by teaching them the thinking tools, so bottlenecks are the result.

This also hurts accountability. A team is more accountable when expectations are set clearly together as a group. If you just tell someone what to do all the time (the "genius with the thousand helpers" model), then they'll robotically carry out the orders, and that becomes the extent of what you can ask of them.

However, if you set the expectations with greater clarity, you can also demand more accountability when they aren't proactively attacking issues.

STOP THE ASSEMBLY LINE

Toyota is well known for the success they had using Total Quality Management (TQM) principles. By the 1970s and 1980s, they were the global leader in high-quality, efficient production standards. Simply put, they were making better cars at a lesser cost than their American counterparts.

One of the keys to their success was empowering all their employees. This was best represented by the andon cord system, where frontline workers could stop the assembly line if they detected a problem. Pulling the cord triggered a signal, alerting the team to the issue. This practice, known as jidoka (automation with a human touch), ensured that quality issues were addressed immediately, rather than allowing defects to continue down the production line.

This specific example may not be directly applicable to your business, but the principle is. Find ways to empower all of your people to identify issues, provide ideas for solutions, and solve them.

CREATING DAILY AWARENESS

The overall aim is to get IDS so deeply into the thinking of your team at every level that they will use this discipline even outside of meetings.

The best way to do that is to make talking and thinking in the language of IDS part of the daily awareness of your team. Exemplify this from the leadership level to get it into the DNA of your culture. It will transform your organization from the inside out.

Tellingly, leaders who successfully integrate IDS deep into their culture turn "IDS" into a verb. "That's an issue that we need to IDS." Or "This project is going off the rails, we need to find time to IDS it in our next L10 Meeting." When it becomes a verb, you know

"everyone is speaking the same language," which is a great sign that your team is healthy.

Another thing for leaders to remember: Ideas from those you employ are free. You are already paying them—why not challenge them for more ideas? Why not create a space for them to get better at calling out issues? Why not stretch their comfort zone so they can reveal friction without fear?

Set the tone: Ideas are free. Encourage people to use their new-found daily awareness to push themselves further. It's a win for the individual and the business. They are developing skills and helping the Greater Good.

WHO–WHO–1 SENTENCE: WHAT IT LOOKS LIKE

Here is an excellent explanation and example from *What the Heck Is EOS?* of the Who–Who–1 Sentence method that we touched on in chapter 4:

WHO. The first "who" is deciding who is raising the issue.

WHO. The second "who" is understanding who is ultimately accountable for solving the issue.

1-Sentence. This means that the person raising the issue must look the person who is accountable for the issue in the eye and state the issue in one sentence—short, sweet, and to the point. No candy-coating.

This is sometimes hard to do, so let's look at an example from a customer-service L10 Meeting.

Meeting Runner: Who is teeing this issue up?

Bob: I am.

Meeting Runner: Who are you talking to?

Bob: Sue.

Meeting Runner: What's the issue in one sentence?

Bob: Sue, I'm not getting reports from you on time.

This is exactly what the process should be like. From here, you can have a productive conversation that might go like this:

Sue: Huh? What are you talking about?

Bob: My customer reports. I need them daily, but I only get them every other day at best. I can't answer my questions if I don't have the most recent reports.

Meeting Runner: I'm not sure we've identified the real issue here. Sue, any idea why Bob is not getting the reports on time?

Sue: Bob, I didn't know you needed them daily. I think that is the real issue. Now that I know, I can send them to you by 9 AM every day. Will that work?

Bob: That would be great.

Sue: I'll take a To-Do to start sending them to you. We can check next week in our L10 and make sure that is working for Bob.

Bob: Great. Thanks, Sue.

Meeting Runner: That issue is solved. On to the next issue. Who's teeing up the next issue?

COMBATING THE ICEBERG
OF IGNORANCE

Leaders should have another motivation to get the Issues Component into the bones of their company culture: so they know what is going on! The reality of running a business, particularly if it has grown to a certain size, is that leaders can sometimes be sitting atop an iceberg of ignorance.

The Leadership Team can see the part of the iceberg sticking out of the water; the rest of the organization knows the bulk underneath. When everyone turns to an observer calling out issues, you are no longer relying on just what you and a handful of leaders can see. No matter how good a leader and observer you may be, you still need an empowered team to help you map the entire iceberg.

EOS Implementer Vincent Bryant shared this example from a team he worked with: "I saw a major retailer that was suffering from major out-of-stock headaches and lost sales for a couple of years. They kept trying to solve it from the board room in top-down style. Finally they explained the problem to the shelf stackers on the front lines and asked them how to solve it. It broke open what was really going on and they were able to fix it."

THE MOST IMPORTANT SKILL

The single most important skill you can teach to your people is the ability to IDS well.

We know that's a big claim, but when you reflect on it, you'll begin to see the truth of it. Issues, at their most basic, are unmet expectations. They are the things standing between where you are and your vision. And these aren't just problems, obstacles, impurities, and challenges. Always remember that issues also include opportunities and new ideas.

When you really get down to it, a vision will always remain a fantasy unless we find ways to solve the obstacles keeping us from it. You can't get there (your vision) from here (where you are now) unless you resolve the issues in the way. And the more successful you are, the more issues you will encounter. It's the nature of the beast, but it's also great fun to keep playing at higher levels.

This skill is also directly linked to accountability. If you can't get clarity on where the friction is and why, how will you ever be accountable for what you can't even clearly define?

You'll never feel so great as when you permanently solve a major issue that has been plaguing your business. The energy released will keep you coming back for more. If you do it enough times, you might just be shocked at the amazing power of removing friction. It will fast-track your growth and ignite your greatness.

* * * * * * * * * * * * * * * * * *

Solving Issues in Real Life

Ingredient: Getting IDS and L10 Meetings to the Entire Company

Ingredient is a food marketing company founded in 1994 that has partnered with various food and beverage brands, including Betty Crocker, Pillsbury, and Lunds & Byerlys, to create content and strategies that connect with consumers.

Business was good for Ingredient and growing. In fact, so good and growing that they made the decision to bring EOS into their business to help sustain it.

Catherine Gillis, Chief Operating Officer of Ingredient, explained the decision.

"We were experiencing rapid growth—about 20 to 25 percent annually for several years—and had just landed a particularly large, complex client. It felt like the right time to become what I jokingly call the 'designated grownups' by putting structure and accountability in place," she said. "Without the tools and framework of EOS, managing that growth would've been a real challenge."

It also brought clarity.

"We got very clear on executive roles, responsibilities, and accountability, which laid the foundation for intentional growth. Defining our vision through the V/TO helped us plan beyond the original partners and set a long-term strategy," Catherine said. "We also refined our Core Values into five clear words—Collaboration, Empathy, Enthusiasm, Adaptability, and Confidence—which everyone in the company now knows by heart."

Ingredient has been successful in rolling out EOS across the entire company, which has had a noticeable impact on the culture—bringing more clarity, consistency, and accountability to how the team works together. Catherine shared that one of the most visible changes has been the way people show up for each other: "There's a different energy when everyone knows what's expected, when we're aligned, and when we have a rhythm we can count on."

One of the key elements driving that rhythm are weekly L10 Meetings. In addition to the Leadership Team meeting, there are also L10s for every department. All 60 Ingredient employees have an L10 that they attend.

"We meet every single week now—everybody in the company is in an L10," Catherine said. That shared cadence, paired with a structured agenda, has helped turn meetings into moments of focus and progress, rather than just check-ins.

The IDS process has become a powerful tool for addressing real issues. "When we first started, people were dropping issues in five minutes before the Leadership Team meeting," she said. "Now I insist they're submitted the day before, with enough detail to actually understand what the problem is."

Catherine reviews the issues ahead of time and starts each IDS section by asking, "What are the hot issues?"—ensuring the team is aligned and ready to dive in. That level of preparation and clarity has elevated how decisions are made and how the team collaborates.

Rolling out weekly meetings and IDS across every team has had a powerful effect on the company culture—especially when it comes to empowering employees.

"People have a regular forum where they can bring up issues," Catherine said. "What it does is push leadership out—teams are solving problems at their level instead of always waiting for leadership to step in." She described how one team, after identifying a challenge in their L10, took the initiative to propose a full restructuring plan on their own before bringing it to the executive team for final review.

This cultural shift has changed the dynamic between employees and leadership. "People are bringing solutions to the executive team more for final vetting and approval instead of waiting for us to solve all the problems—which is amazing," Catherine said.

EOS has also given the company a consistent process for actually addressing problems, especially sensitive ones. "Previously, people issues would linger because we didn't have a process to deal with them. Now we make decisions in a timely manner, and that builds trust with the whole team."

Each group manages its own Issue List, allowing them to focus on what's relevant while giving the executive team space to handle higher-level challenges. As Catherine put it, EOS and the Issues Component have become a foundation for building a stronger, more accountable culture.

CONCLUSION

Our journey through these pages has had one goal: transforming your business into an issues-solving machine by showing you how to remove friction, fast-track your growth, and ignite your greatness.

Learning to solve issues fast and permanently is one of the most transformative things you can do for your team and your business. The way to do this is completely clear, and it's proven. You obsess over and master two tools: the Issues List and the Issues Solving Track. Do this well and it will revolutionize how your team tackles every challenge, obstacle, opportunity, and idea.

Recall that issues will always be there. In fact, the better you get at solving issues, the more you grow, and the more you grow, the bigger the issues. Every dragon you tame, every opportunity you jump on faster, creates momentum that propels your business forward. Great teams realize this truth and look forward to solving issues, because they know it means they are fueling growth.

All this grows in a culture grounded in openness, honesty, and transparency. (If your team needs to develop in this area, return to chapter 2.) Create a culture where trust is high and conflict is healthy, a team that lives Fearless Accountability, where team members care about the Greater Good more than protecting their own turf.

Now it's time to take action.

What's on your Issues List? Fill it up, and then prioritize your top three and go!

. . . .

Solving Issues in Real Life

E-Z Bel Construction: The Freedom of an Issues List

E-Z Bel Construction performs civil and commercial construction projects for a variety of public and private entities. E-Z Bel primarily builds in the San Antonio and South/Central Texas region, specializing in street, drainage, utility, concrete, bridge, and traffic signal work.

Stephen Park joined E-Z Bel Construction in 2011 as a project manager. It was supposed to be the first step of what he jokingly refers to as an "arranged marriage."

"The company was founded by Roy Rodriguez in 1971, and in the early 1990s his son Michael took over. Eventually, Michael was ready to exit the business too," Stephen said.

So a plan was hatched for the "arranged marriage." The idea was to have Stephen and a husband-and-wife pair combine into a team to run the business as Michael eased out of the top role.

It did not work out. Stephen said it led to some toxic situations, and the married couple left. Stephen eventually found himself in the top slot, but without enough knowledge. "I could run a project," he said. "But I had no idea how to run a company."

In 2015, he read the book *Traction* by Gino Wickman, and he saw a good path forward. That September, he had his first conversation with EOS Implementer Jill Young, and things began to improve rapidly.

"One thing I learned looking back is that there is a difference between a Leadership Team that is smart, and one that is smart AND healthy," Stephen said. He went on to explain that a smart Leadership Team can accomplish things and even find some success, but that without healthy interactions, the results will always be less than they should be. Not to mention all the pain that comes from simmering resentments and screaming matches.

"Smart companies can run the right policies and operate in the right markets," he said. "But if you don't have the health component, it makes it that much more difficult to get those same results."

Michael said the team is now healthy, which he describes this way: "When I think of healthy, I just think about a Leadership Team that's willing to be really open and honest about everything. They're able to ask for help when they're struggling. They're able to go into what feels like the danger zone. People are okay with accepting feedback that might sting a little bit. There's no politicking or offline conversation. People are able to address and call out issues."

Figuring out the Issues Component has been a big part of E-Z Bel's success.

Stephen singled out the Issues List as one of his favorite tools because it has given him freedom as the CEO and Visionary.

"For me personally, it's liberating because I have that trait that I see a lot of things, I have a lot of ideas, and I am seeing them all the time," he said. "Now I can just say, 'Oh, just put it on the Issues

List and I know we will deal with it.' Anything that doesn't feel right, even if it is something I can't completely define, I don't worry about it. It just goes on the Issues List."

The Issues List has also helped foster a culture of courage inside E-Z Bel:

"It's the number one step in dealing with issues or opportunities," he said. "The first step has always been that we had somebody at some point that had the courage to put it on the Issues List," Stephen said. "And knowing that the framework is there takes away some of the pressure of it all."

Stephen sums it up this way: "Since we've been operating on EOS, we've tripled revenue, we've tripled headcount, we've substantially improved profitability. So I'm all in on EOS."

CHECKLISTS, TEMPLATES, AND TOOLS

This section has impactful resources to help you reduce friction and fast-track growth. Use them to keep you on track as you create an issues-solving machine inside your business.

ISSUES COMPONENT FAQs

1. **What does IDS stand for in EOS?**
   IDS stands for Identify, Discuss, and Solve. It's the core Issues Solving Track in EOS.

2. **How do you use IDS in a Level 10 Meeting?**
   During the Issues segment of a Level 10 Meeting, the team prioritizes issues and then works through them using the IDS process: Identify the root cause, Discuss the issue thoroughly, and Solve it with a specific action.

3. **What's the difference between Discuss and Solve in IDS?**
   Discuss is about openly sharing perspectives and information, while Solve means agreeing on a clear action that resolves the root issue.

4. **How do you know if you've truly solved an issue in IDS?**
   An issue is solved when the team agrees on a specific action that addresses the root of the issue, not just the symptoms.

5. **What if we don't solve every issue on our list during IDS?**
   It's common not to solve every issue. Focus on the most important ones, and carry unresolved issues forward to the next meeting.

6. **Can IDS be used outside of Level 10 Meetings?**
   Yes, IDS can be used in any meeting or situation where issues need to be solved, including quarterly sessions or departmental meetings.

7. **What are the common mistakes teams make with IDS?**
   Common mistakes include solving symptoms instead of digging to the root of the real issue, letting discussions drag on, or not holding someone accountable for the solution.

8. **How do you prioritize issues for IDS?**

   The team quickly prioritizes issues one, two, and three by simply stating which they believe is most important. The first person to speak claims issue one, the next to speak up takes issue two, and another names issue three. (Or the same person can call out all three issues—this isn't about taking turns!) Don't waste time voting or debating—come ready to speak up for the issue you need solved. On a healthy team, this should take about 15 seconds.

9. **What's the difference between an issue and a to-do?**

   An issue is something that is still not resolved or for which a solution has not been agreed to. A to-do comes after a team has IDS'd an issue and has agreed on a Solve. The to-do is a 7-day action that the team has agreed to, with one person owning the action that will be done in seven days.

10. **How do I know the issue is really solved if we only rely on a 7-day to-do to Solve it?**

    The only reason a team will IDS an issue is to get unstuck on something, or to get agreement and alignment on something. The 7-day to-do gives everyone on the team assurance that the Solve is moving forward.

11. **Should I keep issues on the Issues List until the to-dos are completed?**

    No. To-dos are issues transformed into actions. Once you have a to-do, remove the issue from the Issues List. If it's not truly solved, it will soon make the list again.

12. **What's the difference between a Rock and an issue?**

    Rocks are agreed-to 90-day high priorities. Issues are things that are not yet solved or committed to. They are still barriers, obstacles, ideas, or opportunities. Often, when an issue is solved, it turns into a Rock.

13. **What do we do if the same issues keep coming back?**
This may mean the true root cause hasn't been solved, or solutions aren't being implemented.

14. **How do we hold people accountable for solving issues?**
Assigning clear owners and specific to-dos with a due date ensures accountability. Also, review to-dos in every Level 10 Meeting to confirm progress and address any barriers to execution.

15. **How much time should we spend on solving issues in meetings?**
EOS recommends spending the bulk of the Level 10 Meeting (60 out of 90 minutes) on IDS.

16. **Can issues be solved outside of meetings?**
Yes, and decisions and solutions should be cascaded to the whole team for transparency and accountability.

17. **How do we keep issue solving from turning personal or assigning blame?**
Focus on solving the business problem for the long-term Greater Good of the company, not assigning fault. Reinforce Core Values and use open, respectful language to maintain a safe, productive environment.

18. **Can we solve multiple issues at once, or should we focus on one at a time?**
For best results, prioritize and tackle issues one at a time.

19. **Why is it important to use data and facts in issue solving?**
Relying on opinions or assumptions can lead to poor solutions. Use objective data from your Scorecard or relevant sources to inform discussions and decisions.

20. **What are the risks of having inconsistent Level 10 Meetings or issue solving cadence?**

    Irregular meetings mean issues pile up, get lost, or lose urgency. Stick to a consistent weekly meeting schedule to keep issues visible and solutions timely.

21. **What if some team members resist implementing agreed-upon solutions?**

    Treat it like an issue, because that's what it is. Put it on the Issues List so you can identify concerns openly, reinforce the reasons for change, and tie solutions back to your Core Values and company vision to build buy-in.

22. **Can you identify an issue that doesn't involve you at all?**

    Yes. Get it on the list of the team that can solve it.

23. **What is the difference between the Issues List on the Level 10 Meeting agenda and the Issues List on the V/TO?**

    The Issues List on the L10 Agenda contains short-term issues. We define "short term" as anything that needs to be solved in the next 90 days. The Issues List on the V/TO is your long-term Issues List, and contains items that can be resolved or committed to in the future.

24. **What do we do with issues that have been on our list for a long time?**

    At least once per quarter, compartmentalize your issues. If something is no longer an issue, delete it. You can do this exercise anytime you feel your Issues List is getting too long.

25. **What do we do when our Issues List is too long?**

    This is another situation where compartmentalizing your issues will help. Use the Compartmentalization Tool you will find in this chapter.

THE 10 COMMANDMENTS OF SOLVING ISSUES

From *Decide! The One Common Denominator of All Great Leaders* by Gino Wickman

1. Thou Shalt Not Rule by Consensus
2. Thou Shalt Not Be a Weenie
3. Thou Shalt Be Decisive
4. Thou Shalt Not Rely on Secondhand Information
5. Thou Shalt Fight for the Greater Good
6. Thou Shalt Not Try to Solve Them All
7. Thou Shalt Live with It, End It, or Change It
8. Thou Shalt Choose Short-Term Pain and Suffering
9. Thou Shalt Enter the Danger
10. Thou Shalt Take a Shot

CHECKLIST: DOES IT BELONG ON THE ISSUES LIST?

Before adding an issue to the Issues List in an organization running on EOS, you and your team may want to consider the following questions to ensure the issue is relevant and actionable.

Is this truly an issue? Clearly define the situation, barrier, idea, opportunity, or obstacle.

- Is this slowing you down, ticking you off, causing friction? Is it a challenge, an idea, or an opportunity?
- Is it a recurring issue or a one-time occurrence?
- How does this issue impact our ability to achieve our V/TO, execute, or live our Core Values?

Does the issue align with our company's vision and goals? Ensure the issue impacts our objectives.

- Which goal, Rock, measurable, process, or deliverable does this impact?
- Does resolving this issue move us closer to our 10-Year Target, 3-Year Picture, 1-Year Plan, or Rocks?
- Does this issue align with our V/TO?

Is it a priority (time sensitive or mission critical)? Determine the urgency.

- Does this need to be solved now, or can it wait?
- What would happen if left unaddressed?
- What is the most impactful thing we should solve?

Can I resolve this myself? Assess accountability and resources to address the issue.

- Do I have accountability for solving this?
- Can the issue be solved by me/my team, or does it require cross-functional input?
- Are there any potential solutions I/we could try before bringing it to the (right) Issues List?

Who else is affected? Identify other people (departments, partners, or customers) impacted.

- Who is impacted by this issue?
- Do they need to be involved in discussing or resolving it?
- Have I communicated with them to gather their perspectives?

What are the potential consequences of not addressing the issue? Consider the risks and impact.

- Does this issue cause a bottleneck, friction, or slow progress?
- Does it have financial, reputational, cultural, or operational risks?
- How would it affect our team/company if left unresolved?

Is additional information needed? Gather necessary data or insights to understand the issue fully.

- What data or metrics do we have that provide clarity on this issue?
- Are there key people who need to provide input before discussing it?
- Have I validated any assumptions about the issue?

Have I documented the issue clearly? Provide a clear one-sentence description of the issue.

- Have I written a simple, specific, one-sentence description of the issue (refer back to models here)?
- Have I identified specifically who I need help from and what I want (what solved looks like)?
- Have I prepared and provided enough information/context about the issue to solve it?

By reflecting on these questions, team members can maintain a focused and efficient Issues List, promoting effective IDSing.

ISSUES SOLVING TRACK™

Here is a succinct summary of the Issues Solving Track taught in this book:

Issues are problems, challenges, or obstacles; opportunities; and new ideas worthy of your attention. They're really anything—good or bad—that your team needs to resolve. With your Issues List completely clarified, start by prioritizing the three most important issues to tackle today. Then, follow this three-step Issues Solving Track™:

STEP 1: IDENTIFY

The stated problem is rarely the real issue.

- You have to dig down to find the **real issue**. Don't move forward until you clearly identify the real issue.
- Once you have identified the real issue, then move to discuss it, and stay laser focused on the real issue until it is solved (no tangents).

STEP 2: DISCUSS

Being completely open and honest, every member of the team shares his or her thoughts, ideas, concerns, and solutions regarding the **real issue**.

- Discuss and debate.
- Get it all on the table, but say it only once. Saying it more than once is politicking.

- When it's all on the table and things are getting redundant, it's time to solve.
- When the **real issue** is clearly and openly discussed and kept in mind, the solution is always simple. That doesn't mean easy, and sometimes it's very hard.

STEP 3: SOLVE

"**Solve**" means agreeing on a plan that will make the issue go away forever. *That* you decide is more important than *what* you decide—so decide!

- The solution must be stated by someone until you hear the sweet sound of agreement.
- Sometimes you will have to go back to the discussion step after the solution is stated and debated.
- Once everyone agrees, or at least can live with the decision, the action step(s) must be assigned to an owner and put on the To-Do List (whether they're confirmed as to-dos or in the future as issues).

On a healthy team, everyone will agree with the solution eight out of ten times. When they don't, put the to-do on the Issues List and bring it back for more discussion. The whole point is that **solving issues is faster than avoiding them**. Not everyone will be pleased with the solution, but as long as it's for the Greater Good of the organization, they must disagree and commit to support the decision. From there, you must have a united front moving forward.

COMPARTMENTALIZING™

1YEAR	90-DAY	7-DAY	ISSUES	
GOALS	ROCKS	TO-DOS	LONG	SHORT
			+90 DAYS	-90 DAYS
			V/TO®	Level 10 Meeting®

When thinking about ALL of the issues in your company, it's helpful to use this Compartmentalization Tool to give each issue a home. Here's how to understand how to compartmentalize:

- The biggest of your issues should go in the **first column**. These will become part of your 1-Year Plan during your annual planning session.
- Other big issues that require a longer focus and more resources will become Rocks and belong in the **second column**. (A Rock is an agreed-upon 90-day high priority.) If an issue becomes a Rock, take it OFF the Issues List. Make sure that your Rocks are moving you toward your 1-Year Plan.
- Other issues will arise during the normal course of business and can be solved with a 7-day to-do. Put these in the **third column**.
- Any issue that doesn't belong in the first three columns stays on the Issues List. Place these in the **fourth column**.

Note also that the fourth column is divided into short term and long term. Issues that can and should be solved in the next 90 days belong under the short-term heading. The long-term heading is for anything that can wait for longer than 90 days to be solved.

The whole point of the Compartmentalization Tool is to separate the issues that are already in Solve mode from the issues that don't have a solution yet. Any issue that is still stuck or NOT in motion goes on the Issues List.

Watch the Compartmentalizing video at:

www.eosworldwide.com/compartmentalize

ANIMALS AND ISSUES

Many EOS clients have some helpful shorthand ways to refer to the concepts in the Issues Component. One of the most light-hearted and effective ways to get the concepts across is to use animal terminology.

Not everyone resonates with it, so if it isn't your thing, ignore this. But if it helps, use it and enjoy.

Sacred Cow: A long-standing belief, process, or person no one questions—often protected without merit. Time to challenge its value.

Elephant in the Room: A big, obvious issue that no one wants to talk about. Calling it out brings it into the open for healthy discussion.

Squirrel: A distraction or tangent that pulls the team off track. Saying "Squirrel!" brings focus back to the issue at hand.

Bull: A reminder to avoid bullying, bulldozing, or BS. This calls out aggressive or inauthentic behavior that hurts team trust.

VISIONARY AND INTEGRATOR EXPLAINED

In a few places in this book, we have used the terms "Visionary" and "Integrator," which are both crucial in understanding EOS. Here is a little more about these seats for those unfamiliar with EOS.

The concept of the Visionary and Integrator seats within an organization is one of the great breakthroughs EOS clients experience.

The Visionary is usually the founder or CEO of the company and an entrepreneurial "spark plug." Other good descriptors for a Visionary are inspirational, solver of big problems, idea generator, closer of big deals, and company vision creator and champion. On the potential downside, Visionaries can struggle to develop people, let go of control, and trust others to do what needs done. They can also struggle to stick with the details and not jump from idea to idea.

The Integrator, sometimes called the president or chief operating officer, has the ability to harmoniously integrate the major functions of the business while managing the day-to-day issues that arise. The Integrator is the glue that holds the people, processes, systems, priorities, and strategy of the company together.

If trust is an issue in your business, the turnaround needs to start with these two foundational roles.

To learn more, the best EOS book on this topic is *Rocket Fuel: The One Essential Combination That Will Get You More of What You Want from Your Business.*

THE POWER OF PRACTICING RADICAL CANDOR + THE SPEED OF TRUST

We have noted several books throughout this text. Here are two more recommendations that complement the ideas you have found in the previous chapters:

KIM SCOTT'S *RADICAL CANDOR*

Kim Scott presents a refreshing, no-nonsense framework for building trust and fostering effective communication in the workplace. At its core, the concept is simple but profound: Great leadership stems from caring personally while challenging directly. It's about two-way feedback that's both kind and honest.

Scott's advocacy for personally caring means showing genuine empathy and treating people as humans, not just resources. She pairs this with the ability to challenge people directly—saying what needs to be said.

You can treat people with Ruinous Empathy, Manipulative Insincerity, Obnoxious Aggression, or Radical Candor. It is candor combined with care that strikes the perfect balance: being clear and honest while demonstrating real concern for the individual.

Replacing "fake niceness" with authentic, direct communication is the kinder option. Addressing issues head-on prevents simmering resentments. Directness is not harsh—it's having enough respect for someone to be clear and honest.

STEPHEN M. R. COVEY'S *THE SPEED OF TRUST*

Stephen M. R. Covey maintains that trust is a critical, measurable asset that dramatically affects the speed and cost of every relationship and transaction—both personal and organizational. When trust is high, speed increases and costs go down. When trust is low, everything slows down and becomes more expensive.

Covey outlines four core elements of trust—Integrity, Intent, Capabilities, and Results—and he emphasizes that trust can be intentionally built and restored. He introduces the idea of the "trust dividend" and "trust tax," illustrating how trust directly affects performance and outcomes.

This book is valuable because it offers practical tools to assess and improve trust at every level—from individuals to teams to entire organizations. Rather than seeing trust as a soft value, Covey reframes it as a strategic advantage, essential for effective leadership, collaboration, and innovation.

THE OFFLINE MEETING TRACK

Even if you are having regular weekly meetings as taught by EOS, additional meetings sometimes will be called for a variety of reasons.

Often, the beginnings of these meetings are very poorly managed, and people spend 15 or more minutes just trying to figure out the meeting's purpose and who is running it. When these meetings do happen, you can eliminate this purposelessness and stop wasting time. Here's how to do it:

(Remember, this doesn't apply to your regular weekly meetings. Those have a set agenda. This is a tool for other meetings.)

The 5 Steps for a Productive Meeting

Step 1: What is the objective?

Whoever is calling the meeting should decide the objective of the meeting in advance. What must be accomplished by the end of this meeting?

Step 2: What is the agenda?

What are the steps and topics you are going to follow and cover to achieve the objective?

Step 3: What prep work needs to be done?

Be clear with everyone in advance as to what work needs to be done prior to the meeting so that everyone comes fully prepared. This will create much more efficient and productive meetings.

Step 4: In advance, send all participants the objective, agenda, and prep work.

Give plenty of prep time.

Step 5: Begin the meeting by stating the objective and the agenda.

Make sure everyone is clear about why you are together and what needs to be accomplished.

PERSONAL ISSUES SOLVING SESSION

Certain special scenarios are best handled separately. One type is when old grudges or clashes surface and become personal. This is a particular danger in family-run businesses where siblings or parent–child relations are in the mix. The family dynamics have bubbled over into the business and are becoming severe. Here, a Personal Issues Solving Session may be called for.

Here is what you do:

- Have a third party facilitate this session (this could be another member of the team or your EOS Implementer).
- Have each person prepare and then share what they think the other person's three greatest strengths and weaknesses are.
- List all of the issues.
- IDS them.
- List the action items from the solutions.
- Meet in 30 days to follow up on the action items.

Ninety percent of the time, this solves the issues between the two people. Other times, they can't resolve their issues; in that case, one of them needs to leave the business.

MENTAL MODELS FOR IDSing

You will recall that in chapter 4 we briefly touched on a few mental models: the lenses we use to make sense of the world and think through issues. Here are some expanded explanations of helpful models.

Keep in mind that none of the following models are intended to be the last word on this subject, and none are strictly necessary to become good at identifying the root of an issue. Use the ones that make sense to you, and skip those that don't resonate.

"WHAT ARE THE INCENTIVES?" MODEL

When you are searching for an ultimate "why," examine how the people that affect the issue are incentivized. It will often tell you everything you need to know.

Of course, money is the big incentive we immediately think of, and it is unquestionably powerful. But we're humans, and it's far from our only incentive. There are all kinds of psychological and emotional incentives too. Put yourself in the shoes of others and ask what is motivating their behavior.

Also, look at the alignment of incentives. Could some of the incentives be conflicting and triggering erratic outcomes? When you get stuck, stop and ask, "What are the incentives here?"

HANLON'S RAZOR MODEL

Hanlon's Razor teaches us that most problems happen because of mistakes, ignorance, or incompetence, not because of bad intentions or conspiracies. People don't usually try to cause harm—it's often just a result of human error or misunderstanding. Recognizing this helps us tackle problems with more clarity and less suspicion.

When faced with underperformance, we often jump immediately to assuming bad intent or attribute it to a lack of alignment with the company's Core Values. Deeper investigation often reveals a different story. Perhaps the person doesn't "Get it, Want it, or have the Capacity" (GWC) for their role.

The mismatch between their skills and the demands of their seat might be the real issue. Alternatively, it could stem from inadequate training or a leader abdicating responsibility, leaving someone overwhelmed and unprepared. Avoid the assumption that attitude or a Core Values mismatch are the root of the problem until you've explored other possibilities.

SECOND-ORDER-THINKING MODEL

Second-order thinking is the practice of looking past immediate outcomes to consider the broader, "down-the-line" effects of decisions or actions.

If you are struggling with an issue, look behind it and ask, "Is the stated issue the real issue?" While first-order thinking stops at the surface—focusing on what happens now—second-order thinking asks, "What happens next? What ripple effects will this choice create?" The more experience you have, the more you will be able to see the long-term consequences of an issue and the better your decisions will get.

Key Principles of Second-Order Thinking:
- **Think Beyond the Immediate:** First-order thinking asks, "What's the direct result of this action?" Second-order thinking probes further: "How will this impact the broader system or situation over time?"

- **Map Out Cause and Effect:** Trace how an initial action might trigger a chain reaction of events.
- **Prioritize Long-Term Outcomes:** Instead of focusing on short-term wins or fixes, evaluate how choices might shape the future.
- **Balance Trade-Offs:** By considering broader implications, second-order thinking helps weigh the hidden costs and benefits of decisions.

Here's how second-order thinking might look like in business strategy: A company might lower prices to attract customers (first-order thinking). Second-order thinking considers whether this might spark a price war and erode profitability across the industry.

TO GO DEEPER

To learn more about specific EOS components, these books can help:

- For more on how to become an expert on processes, check out the book *Process! How Discipline and Consistency Will Set You and Your Business Free* by Mike Paton and Lisa González.
- To learn more about mastering the People Component, see *People: Dare to Build an Intentional Culture* by Mark O'Donnell, Kelly Knight, and CJ DuBe.
- To improve your Data Component, read *Data: Harness Your Numbers to Go from Uncertain to Unstoppable* by Mark O'Donnell, Angela Kalemis, and Mark Stanley.

ACKNOWLEDGMENTS

Everyone has issues. Everyone has ideas, obstacles, barriers, and opportunities. We all face new things that become unresolved every day. As a result, I believe this book is the most important book I've written to date, and it wouldn't have been possible without my coauthors, Jill Young and Sue Hawkes. They are amazing and powerful women who added tremendous value to the creation of this work.

Many powerful women have helped me on my journey as a leader and an entrepreneur. I would not be an EOS Implementer without CJ Dube's constant mentoring, encouragement, and promotion. I also want to thank my business partner at EOS Worldwide, Kelly Knight, for her persistence and dedication to moving the cause of EOS forward on our way to 100,000+ companies running on EOS with an EOS Implementer. To my mom, Rita O'Donnell, who created an environment that forced me to solve my own issues at a young age.

Thank you, Gino Wickman, for reviewing the manuscript and helping make the book great, and thank you to all the test readers in the EOS Implementer community for providing stories and input.

Thanks to the EOS Worldwide team, especially Hannah Helmholdt and Amber Baird, for moving the writing process forward.

Also, thanks to David Moffitt for guiding Jill, Sue, and me through the process and herding these out-of-control visionaries to create something of tremendous value.

Finally, to you, the reader. You are the changemakers. You create everything around us and make the world a better place. Remember, *"it's just an issue."*

—Mark O'Donnell

Gino Wickman and Don Tinney for wisdom, guidance, and the great big dent you've made in the world and my life.

Dan Hawkes and our shared EOS Implementer community who make us all better.

Our kids, Ali, Quinton, and Summer, who are amazing examples of all that is possible. Thank you, Q, for sharing your talent by illustrating this book!

Our clients, who have taught me that the real magic happens when trust and teamwork align—you become unstoppable.

—Sue Hawkes

Thank you to my clients, for trusting me not only to lead you, but to learn alongside you. You've been my real-time test lab, letting me try, tweak, and experiment in the moments that have mattered most. Because of you, I've grown as a coach, as a leader, and as a human, and I've discovered that a little curiosity and courage can move mountains.

To my community of Wise Women, you are my sounding board, my source of inspiration, and my constant support. Your wisdom and friendship have carried me through the highest highs and the toughest challenges. I am endlessly grateful.

To the EOS Implementers I talk with daily, thank you for IDS-ing with me in real time, swapping ideas, and offering unfiltered support. Your hand-holding, encouragement, and generosity have been the background to so many of my wins. You've shown me that collaboration isn't just smart, it's downright enchanting!

And finally, thank you to the dinner tables of the world. For so many of us entrepreneurs, the dinner table was more than a place to eat. It was the first boardroom, the first classroom, and the site of our earliest issue-solving sessions. It's where parents talked about clients and payroll alongside math homework and mashed potatoes. It's where the realities of running a family business sat side by side with running a family . . . the steady foundation of so much personal and professional growth.

—Jill Young

ABOUT THE AUTHORS

Mark O'Donnell is the Visionary and CEO of EOS Worldwide and an Expert EOS Implementer®. A lifelong entrepreneur, he has founded and sold multiple businesses and coached more than 100 companies on their journey to achieving what they want from their business. Mark's passion is helping people live their EOS Life®—doing what they love, with people they love, making a difference, being compensated appropriately, and having time for other passions.

As Visionary of EOS Worldwide, Mark is on a mission to help one million people transform their lives using the tools of the Entrepreneurial Operating System®. A lifelong learner, he studied at Albright College, Northeastern University, and The Wharton School at the University of Pennsylvania. He lives outside Philadelphia, Pennsylvania, with his wife, Rachel, their three children, his mother-in-law, and their 100-pound dog, Blue.

Sue Hawkes started her first business at age 10, selling door-to-door with her best friend. She's upgraded her offerings since then, but she's always been obsessed with helping people and solving problems. Today, Sue helps high achievers create winning cultures where accountability thrives. She gracefully tackles the tough stuff while clearing any friction that slows people (and profits) down. Sue is a keynote speaker, best-selling author, Certified Business and Executive Coach, CEO of YESS!, and Expert EOS Implementer®. If there is friction in your company, she'll help you name it, face it, and solve it—for good. Sue brings the tools and the truth-telling to help you transform your business challenges permanently, without wasting time. Sue has regularly been featured in *Forbes*, *Fast Company Inc.*, and *Entrepreneur*, and has earned numerous leadership awards for her transformational work with companies across the globe. She's here to help you stop avoiding what's hard, lean into what matters, and lead like you mean it—with clarity, purpose, and just enough humor to make it all stick.

Jill Young is best known for her ability to lift and encourage teams in inspiring and creative ways, or as she calls it, MAGIC! Since 2014, she has coached hundreds of leadership teams as an EOS Implementer based in Dallas, Texas. She is the author of The Advantage Series, a collection of books to help leadership teams become their best; the Creatrix of Coaching Magic, a school for passionate and dedicated coaches; and she served as head coach of EOS Worldwide. Jill loves cocreating projects (like this book!), leading active workshops, and facilitating transformational experiences. Connect with Jill at JillYoung.com.

ENTREPRENEURIAL
OPERATING SYSTEM®

BECOME AN
EOS IMPLEMENTER®

Apply your entrepreneurial skills in a whole new way by joining our growing community of 850+ EOS Implementers around the world.

EOS Implementers live their best lives by helping entrepreneurs live theirs. They walk the walk, talk the talk, and have an incredible network of businesses who thrive by running on EOS.

If you've got what it takes to be a talented coach, teacher, and facilitator, and you're ready to start a new chapter by bringing EOS® to the world, maybe your next career move is becoming an EOS Implementer.

Find out today at: **EOSFRANCHISING.COM**